KEYS TO OUR WOES

A Reasonable Evolutional Idea
and Solution to Mental Health

ETERNAL ME

Table of Contents

Inviting All to Join The Discussion

Eternal-Me has written many of his surveyed discussions that have taken place over the last 10–11 years of incarceration. 17 years ago Eternal-Me had encounters to some awaking of higher self-awareness. Now, he intends to give back to the world, and all who would be willing to receive its beauty of love, with the release of these discussions.

The intended goal and contribution to release these sensible discussions is to create an evolutional effect on earth. To the return of Eden, to end our collective immunity to the mental encumbrance and deterioration we're all confronted with. These discussions are especially designed to lift the illusional veil that has been ritually practiced. A false belief that many have allowed themselves to perceive and believe—that they themselves or any societies on our world are of some sort of collective mental normality.

We all have our own personal mental disorder or delusions. It has only been a matter of some measures and degrees that some of us are more operational than others. Nevertheless, we have always been, we are and always will be collectively in participation with humanity's evolving transition to a higher mental conscious stature.

There are five different discourses that can reveal the associated mental connections and practicalities to one's inner comprehension of such an advanced mental health discussion and concept.

Shall we now observe and inquire into this key to our woes? Let's begin.

Keys to Our Woes

Introduction

The Rapture

The Foretelling Rapture

There is a prevalent and traditional perspective pertaining to the foretelling concept and word "rapture." There have been multitudes of mainstream Christian interpretations passed down on the term. The most common translation associated with the word rapture has been the popular doomsday interpretation that targets the lower ego's delusional dysfunctions, ones of fear of some sort of harm encountered. A harm done to the individual self (ego). Some religious traditionalists believe rapture is a fear of the thought of being left behind to face the great tribulation, or just simply losing a loved one from the encounter of just being "caught up" to the heavens and onto a physical paradise, which still has the misconception victimization effect to one's ego, feelings and human experiences. A mundane perspective that only panders to the lower ego.

"The great tribulation" is a phrase in the Bible that pertains to a prophetic prediction at a time of great mental and physical affliction and hardship in the world. The phrase "caught up," as well as the great tribulation, are Bible phrases that decipher the word "apocalypse." It is a phrase that stems from the Greek word apokalupsis. It describes the events of the world and one's debilitating end, destruction and disaster, as well as the destruction and end of all of humanity and the world. The great tribulation and the encounter of being caught up are associated with the word rapture (to be caught up). To be raptured (in the Oxford dictionary), is to transport in delight, euphoria, ecstasy, joy and bliss. It is not to say the nations and the world will not one day experience a physical and external great tribulation and end. However, the apokalupsis that also embodies the involvement of the rapture will or may have occurred at any time in the past or future, and will or may transpire at our current time and moment. To be caught up and raptured describes one's achievements to higher consciousness and mental maturity, even in the midst of destruction and total mayhem. A planetary rapture advanced upon the inhabitants of a nation and our world allows the growth of human affairs to supersede our ongoing jointed undeveloped mental position.

Intended Objective

I am describing the word rapture in order to engage in conversation with my fellow human family and loved ones all around the world, in regards to our common approach and observation on how we deal with matters of our mental conditions and complexities. The objective purpose of this conversation is for all to contribute intuitively and reasonably, heartfelt and loving contributions to such a discussion. This conversation is intended with the utmost love and respect for all humanity. The ongoing psychological state we are all interlocked in has caused us to reevaluate our human purpose. By way of connecting to one's inner works, the development that connects to the discovery of the simplest solution to mend our world's mental, spiritual and physical inefficiencies has led to a clear logical resolution. This is where the word rapture comes into play.

To Alter the Procedure to the Goal of Rapture

Conditions, circumstances, environments, more effective mental elevations and a rapture can all be manufactured. With a different approach other than prisons being the primary replacement for mental asylums, we can seek a broader progressive and productive approach.

In Woodford County, Illinois, a state attorney charged a nine-year-old, without delay, with five counts of first degree murder, two counts of arson, one count of aggravated arson with a one-year-old, two two-year-olds, a 34-year-old man and a 69-year-old woman.

A very tragic incident for all affected and involved. However, to respond to an undeveloped, nine-year-old mind and troubled child with an impulsive decision can only indicate that our governmental bureaucratic establishments have some mentally unstable positions and practices that we may all need to reexamine in order to seek out a more improved and advanced approach to such matters. Especially when a nine-year-old, let alone any other human being no matter the crime, is sanctioned to savage prison institutions with substantial pharmaceutical influences. These so-called reformatory installations are pitiful and unproductive. They are only structured to recycle mental inefficiencies.

To be caught up in the rapture is to also achieve the highest measure of mental sanity. The rapture and mental sanity is the purpose for all humanity.

In order to accomplish this mental rapture, we must all awaken to the possibility of a massive mental rapture for humanity. We must awaken to the idea in order to discover the evolution of our true selves. Let us explore some circumstantial measures to the consideration of such a vision.

Awaken to the Idea of a Solution

A Manufactured Rapture (Higher State of Consciousness)

An Awakening

Many come, and many have come to awaken man from the perceived profound psychotic, delusional, mental and spiritual paralysis that we all experience.

On account of our current state of the world and nationwide chaotic mental discrepancies, we tend to apply repetitious remedies to matters that do not necessarily result in the effect of healing, or a sufficient cure to our current state. So, is there a chance of a psychological awakening of the matter?

Gratification is an imperative principle to the great masterful sources of our higher awakening. However, until we initiate the application of masterful principles, higher awakening principles may not essentially be attainable for us here, in our present mental state. The indication of this unattainable awakening stems partially from our diminishing acceptability to the requirements of advance awakening.

The word "perceived" I used before is key. According to an individual's perceptional position on their circumstances in life, he or she may have a restricted response to his or her intake on day-to-day experiences, which is also relevant to the equivalence of our current state of mental desensitization, of self and world suffering. Perception is critical and key to our awakening.

Higher awakening must be measured by its result. So, let's take a look at our present state of mainstream religion.

The Result of Religion

You could possibly say, "what have you done for us, where are your results?" True religion is determined by its effect—not only in the individual, but also on the masses. It is the outcome of religion in its current state that turns many astray. Although, at the same time, it is not so much religion that is at fault for man's loss of interest in and misguidance away from religion as it is man's minimal understanding of religion. This limited aspect of religion is caused by restricted truth, or a restricted understanding of truth, that allocates the confinement of the actions and result of truth. Truth is truth because it appropriates irrefutable conclusive fact. Truth is actual and truth is absolute being. Truth is experiencing and inexperiencing certainty. The experiences of truth will get us to the point of being conscious of truth, and the awareness that consciousness is who we are and that we are all the same consciousness, which will result in no more conflict between each other once we see only the truth. There will be only our harmonious flow. All of our differences between each other will then be irrelevant.

Truth is a matter of therapeutic inner experiencing. The promise and expectation of mainstream religion in my assessment have been inattentive. So, how could this be so? By evidence we all see in our mass mental dysfunctional paralysis that's separating us all from the truth.

Evidence that Witness our Mass Mental Paralysis

Mental paralysis is when the mind recycles crippling undeveloped responses to thoughts, actions and circumstance without a maturing and evolutional reckoning to whatever thoughts, action and circumstance one recycles.

As an individual exercising purpose in the bigger blueprint of mass purpose, here is my witness and evidence of our mass mental paralysis. Just to name a few: we encounter wars, political corruption and gridlock, police brutality and law enforcement corruption, public shootings, domestic and foreign terrorism. We see the normalization of multiple measures of violence, business and corporate corrupt practices, mass incarceration, and the acceptance of poverty. America has a very broken justice system structured on the practice of retribution, with an unclear use of the word fair and justice, conventionally used under false pretenses. The term mental paralysis recounts the psychological veil and mental shutdown humanity endures, causing the effect of doing nothing to resolve this consequence we all tend to witness. Under our true nature, we would engage in practical resolutions to these consequences.

Collective Participation

So yes, I get it, you're probably saying to yourself, "This inventory of symptoms has been around, and always will be around." However, even this particular observation of mental impaired traditionalism should also be considered the witness and evidence of all of our madness, because it normalizes our collective mental and conscious position that has brought us all to our current collective mental dysfunctional paralysis. There is nothing normal about our world's current mass mental conditions. Yes, I say "us all" because we are all in this together, whether we agree on the matter or not, or whether we're able to see our current state as it is or not. Whether we like it or not, we're all in this together. We are all one man. That means we all affect each other in many ways. In order to overcome our mass mental paralysis, we must all begin with self-accountability. Many experience insanity as doing the same thing repetitiously expecting different results, only to arrive at the same conclusion. So, in our present collective psychological state, via evidence in one's assessment of universal law, we are all partaking in the state of insanity.

The Normalization of Mental Paralysis

So here we are—humanity, all over the globe, but especially in America in our present condition, where we reduce our standards on how we determine, measure or perhaps diagnose this collective mental dysfunctional state. How? By perceiving what we do and do not do, in regards as the regular norm. We collectively reveal our insensitivity to this prevalent state of being dysfunctional. The nature and law of the nature of how we're responding to our ongoing psychological norms, day in and day out is reciprocating a cause-and-effect of the matter,

8

which is culminating this predicament we are in the center of. Such as the political climate, racial tensions, and an ineffective health care struggle. This all evenly balances out to the mentally dysfunctional, voting into political positions one of their very own, someone who's mentally dysfunctional. The law of the nature of this particular mass psychological dysfunctionality indicates an inevitable tumultuous increase of such a dysfunction, possibly never before imagined. It divulges with the power of magnetism. We are in the midst of a cycle that's considered impracticable to overcome if there is no response.

When a public terrorist shooting or some type of terrorist encounter from an American citizen occurs, we hear many people, even news anchors, repeating the same remarks: "why did this happen, is this the new norm, and how did this happen?" These questions alone testify to us all being mentally disassociated and paralyzed. Though the answer to these mental matters is undeniably clear.

The Idea

So please allow me to elaborate what could be discerned as a very peculiar perspective. A position, possibly envisioned as simplistic: we all must begin to advocate for a mental health care system that is concentrated and centered on the whole. Not just for the incarcerated or those diagnosed with some sort of mental impediment at the present moment, but for the whole, for the masses. Every citizen, resident and person, from the President of the United States of America, to the sanitation worker or the maid worker, should be subject to a mental health and wellness treatment system for all. We must begin to advocate for such a system.

Now I know it may seem a bit of an extreme kind of approach or proposition, but if there is any ability to exercise rationality toward the matter of our current state, you could possibly establish a justification of this idealistic importance. So I say yes—there is a chance of a psychological awakening, with a mental health and wellness treatment system for all, that could get us all to a rapture.

Understanding the Five Discourses
(In Order to Comprehend the Idea of an Awakening)

Let's analyze a few spiritual discourses that could transmit us to a broader vantage point. It is the limited angles of understanding of these subjects that have a hand in our shape and health of impression.

KEYS TO OUR

WOES

The Five Discourses

The Keys

GOD?

The Word God

There are many nuances and subtleties of the word "God." It is a word that has an unlimited number of chronicles that could be regarded at times as contradicting. The word God has been a very, very complex word for humanity throughout history, and even up to this present moment. Our limited perspectives on the topic and word God are due to traditional interpretations bound by many conditions of traditionalism. This is caused when the intellect is stirred by the lower ego, which results in the distortions of truth on the subject of God. There have been many misleading religious practices in the name of God. In many occasions, misleading instructors of light (of the knowledge of the universe), through their misguided practices of deceit, have broadened the distortions of the word God that have dwelt with us to this present moment.

This word God has been humanized, which leads to a narrow sentiment on this subject of discourse.

Dimensional Discernment

Now what I mean by stating that the word has been humanized is that there is and always has been a third dimensional prospect of this essential word. The content of the third dimension is deemed in the higher dimensions as the delusional realm. We, as human beings, with external governing perspectives, have been stalled in this delusional third dimensional discernment. So we delusionally humanize our perception of the word God because we only view the word in a third dimensional assessment.

We're unable to fathom the fourth elemental conscious self without an indispensable measure of discerning the definition of the word God. The comprehension of one's self gives us the advantage of containing a wholesome mental balance. So without the comprehension of the word God, there is the equivalent of a deficiency of understanding one's self, and vice versa. To comprehend one's self is to understand the word God.

Definition

In the book of Exodus, Exodus 3:13-14 it reads:

> *Then Moses said to God, "Indeed, when I come to the children of Israel and say to them; 'The God of your fathers has sent me to you,' and they say to me, 'what is His name?' What shall I say to them?" And God said to Moses, "I Am who I Am." And He said, "Thus you shall say to the children of Israel, 'I Am has sent me to you.'"*

Well, this describes the definition of the word God as: I Am. If you were to look these two words up, the word "I" refers to self. The word "Am" means being or to be. The word "being" or "to be" means exist. That equates the definition of the word God to mean: I Am existence, period. Some believe the evidence of God is a haze in pseudoscience, although the evidence is existence itself. Due to the fact that the definition of the word God is existence, who can deny the evidence we all experience, since we all are experiencing existence?

Other definitions and descriptions, such as God being Omnipotent (meaning all powerful) Omniscient (meaning all knowing) and Omnipresent (meaning all present everywhere), can be included in a vantage point I define as, "super reasonable." Super reasoning is experienced through one's intuition.

In the process of reasoning, there are numerous powers indescribably mysterious to our current comprehension. Super reason could interpret all powers in the totality of the universe and existence as omnipotent. If super reason can interpret all information as endless, then super reason can also interpret all infinite information of the spirit and character of existence, detected and yet to be determined as omniscient. In the process of reasoning, if God is all existence, then even in the thought of the general notion of infinite being, super reason interprets all existence, which is God as Omnipresent.

Everything sensed, touched, felt and experienced is God. Every dream, delusion, expression, and dimensional expression, is what we call God. Every human being is God. God is the teacher and the student. Law and principle is God. Nature is God. Any concept you could possibly think of is God. Rabbi Moses Cordovero describes in the Kabbalah practice that there is nothing outside of existence, but existence only. Nothing could be, without it existing in existence, which is God. Even love is God.

This is the interpretation that super reasonably transmits an explanation that God is in all places at the same time, because God is all places, and all things. To see pantheistically—(God in and as all things)—could perhaps more likely alter behaviors.

Descriptions of Existence and God's Characteristic Dimensions

Many call God the Father, the Universe, Yahweh, Allah, Jehovah, Brahma or Spirit, and many other names.

Spirit

However, the word "spirit" is used for the most part to describe the experience and attributes of existence. The one definition that describes spirit well is character. This is why we use the phrase, "the spirit of something, the spirit of love, the spirit of peace," et cetera. It is to express the persona or character of someone or something. To be a spiritual person is to operate in the awareness of the characteristics of the higher conscious self (God) that purifies and strengthens the mind and body of one's spiritual journey toward the essence of one's higher mental state. In Christianity, spirit is recounted as God the Father, the Son and the Holy Spirit. Each possessing multiple dimensional characteristics. There is also God the Absolute, God the Ultimate, God the Supreme and God the Sevenfold.

There are measures of comprehending the dimensions of the characteristics of spirit. To tune into those measures is like tuning into radio frequencies, but only through the implementation of spirit's characteristics of nature and laws. Spirit is all there is, was and will be.

The Holy Spirit

The characteristic known as the Holy Spirit is an intercessor. It communicates the word (The Son or universal knowledge), through our dreams, feelings, memory, visions and images that are experienced through the intuition. The Holy Spirit is the creation vibration. It is also called the AUM vibration. The AUM vibration is a characteristic of the Holy Spirit some call the Shakti that makes every existing experience move and dwell. The Holy Spirit could intercede, internally and externally. It is also depicted as the Divine Mother.

The Son

The character known as the Son is the awareness of the word (the knowledge of the universe) and it is the word. The word is spirit, character and life. The Son, which is the word, is the knowledge and character of the Father. Jesus said to his disciples in John 14:6 "I am the way, the truth, and the life. No one comes to the Father except through me." Now the Son (the Word), which is also called Universal Consciousness, is also a level of consciousness that must imperatively be at completion, in order to accomplish the abode and the realization of the father (the Cosmic Consciousness).

The Father

The character known as the Father is also known as Cosmic Consciousness, or as stated before, the absolute, or existence period. It is the prime character. The Father is the Son and the Holy Spirit. It is the comparison of possessing a brain, heart and senses.

The essence, the fundamental nature, paradise, the center of the Father (Cosmic Consciousness), who is also called Spirit, is the ecstasy or bliss known as the Father. It is the joy of the Lord the Bible alludes to. Love and light nourish the bliss, and the bliss feeds love and light. This exchange sustains the infinite bliss. The bliss moves out and inward of the center of the Father, and its centrality is omnipresent, omniscient and omnipotent.

The Map of God & the Trinity

The map of God describes some key functional dimensional characteristics of who, what, and where we are in this universe. So let's begin with the center of the circles.

The Center Circles

The first and center circle we shall call the great "I Am" that I have described previously also known as the Bliss, Existence, the Father, the Absolute, SAT (identified in the Bhagavad Gita), and Cosmos or Cosmic Consciousness.

This particular dimension and realm is the highest realm of what we call Paradise, Heaven, Eden, and the Kingdom. It is the Absolute, the seed and the head of all there is. It is the dimension and realm we are all on the voyage back to the consciousness and state of.

The second circle from the center dimension and realm is called "Universal Consciousness," (also the Son, TAT (identified in the Bhagavad Gita), Christ Consciousness, the Word). It is the realm we also call Paradise, Heaven, Eden and the Kingdom. It is the dimension and realm and character of the center circle and the Absolute. It is the realm of creation. As mentioned before, in order to reach, understand and dwell in the highest realm of Cosmic Consciousness or what we call the Father, one must accomplish the dimension and realm of Universal or Christ Consciousness.

The third circle and dimensional realm is called "Om (identified in the Bhagavad Gita), the creation vibration." The Christians of Christianity call it the Holy Spirit or the Witness. It is also known by many as the Power of Consciousness and mother God. It is also the realm known as Paradise, Heaven, Eden and the Kingdom. It is the dimension and character of the center circle and the Absolute. The realm of the AUM (also written Om) vibration is the cause of every, any and all movement and actions of existence. It is the force and the power that makes universal conscious creations, conscious thought or word, and the world come to life. It delivers, with vibration, the magnetic attraction to the unconscious consciousness. In order to reach universal and cosmic consciousness, one must tune into this vibrating force (called the Shakti in the realm of Hinduism) and witnessing force (called the Shiva in the realm of Hinduism) by way of using one's intuition and super reasonable capabilities in exercising the principles of one's self-awareness and self-reflection.

The outer realms outside of the dimensions and realms of paradise that still have the accessibility to the characteristics of the realms of paradise and the Absolute cosmos are called the "Super Universes," which dwell where the measures of maya (the delusional realms) are inhabited. It is where the lower ego that identifies with the physical and individual body and self encounters the delusions of the physical universe. The outer realm of maya and the lower ego is the physical universe. The physical realm is the universe of karma.

The realms of the Father, the Son and the Holy Spirit are known in the Hindu and Eastern Hemisphere faiths as SAT, TAT, AUM or Brahma, Vishnu and Rudra, the trinity of creation, sustenance and destruction combined as one. They are omnipresent even in the outer delusional realms. They are Absolute and unlimited, personal and impersonal. This is why the outer realms remain identified as the cosmos, or I Am.

The seven dimensions of the cosmos and I Am is where we have already discussed the Father, the Son and the Holy Spirit of the seven dimensions in the first and center, second and third circles.

God the Absolute is the final level to progress the individual unification and expansion to oneself as the unlimited beginningless, endless Absolute.

God the Supreme is all creation with I Am awareness as one mind.

God the Ultimate is the realizations of the identifying manifestations of God identified as His created creatures in created events that are time and space transcendent.

God the Seven Fold are the gate keeping of the super universes and the first creature level of supreme being that identifies the creature as a creator identity in the Supreme Being.

The human conscious measures begin with the mind. Thought and the mind are the same. Thought is consciousness condensed as the mind. The mind abides with the lower ego, until it has been liberated by the devotional practices of purifying the mind back to pure consciousness.

The subconscious state is when the mind is conscious of thoughts and feelings though not fully aware and sensed of. The lower ego or unsettled mind can set in motion a subconscious encounter, according to one's karmic measured position. The subconscious state is activated as well, through repetitious behavior.

The conscious measure is when the awareness of the intuitive inner work begins to enter the experience of recognizing one's true higher cosmic self in all there is.

The super conscious state is when the intuitive inner works and witness (the Sheva, the witnessing characteristics of the Holy Spirit) subdue the lower ego in preparation for fourth dimensional insight and beyond.

The universal conscious state is when the devotional practice of purifying one's mind merges with a complete intuitive witnessing insight of higher dimensional perspectives of the kingdom, and both have reached their measure just before the cosmic stages initiation.

The cosmic conscious state is when the universal conscious state has reached its completion, and becomes initiated and transformed permanently with the final stage to merge in unification with God, the Absolute and highest self.

The awareness of one's true self, which is one's absolute highest self seems to be a wise direction to cater to. A mental health and wellness treatment system for all can provide humanity with a roadmap to one's mentally balanced higher self.

THE EXTERNAL REALMS OF THE
CIRCLES OF ABSOLUTE
CONSCIOUSNESS
AND COSMIC POWERS

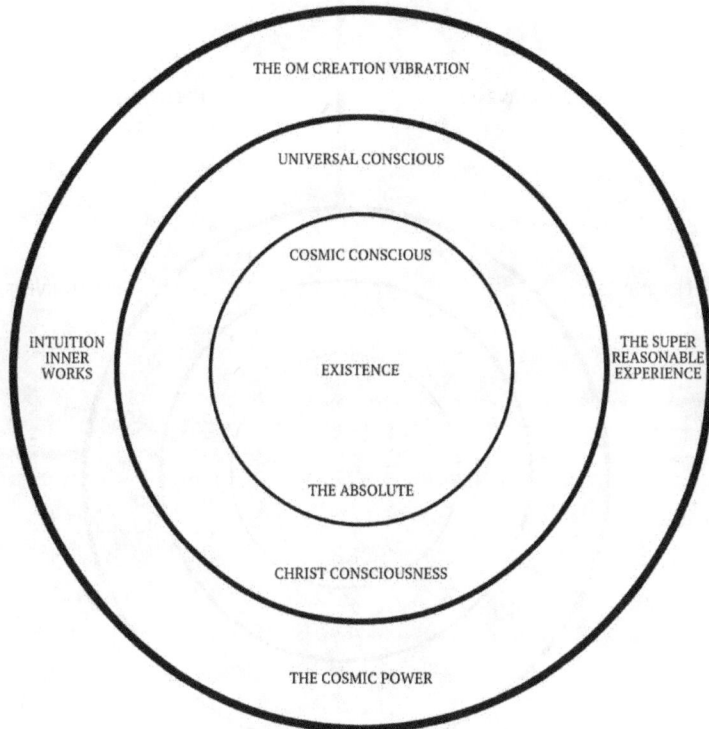

THE OM CREATION VIBRATION

UNIVERSAL CONSCIOUS

COSMIC CONSCIOUS

INTUITION
INNER
WORKS

EXISTENCE

THE SUPER
REASONABLE
EXPERIENCE

THE ABSOLUTE

CHRIST CONSCIOUSNESS

THE COSMIC POWER

SUPER UNIVERSES

MAYA
THE DELUSIONAL
REALMS

EGO
THE IDENTIFICATION
WITH THE BODY

THE PHYSICAL REALM IS THE
UNIVERSE OF KARMA WHERE MAYA
AND THE LOWER EGO DWELLS OUTSIDE
OF PARADISE

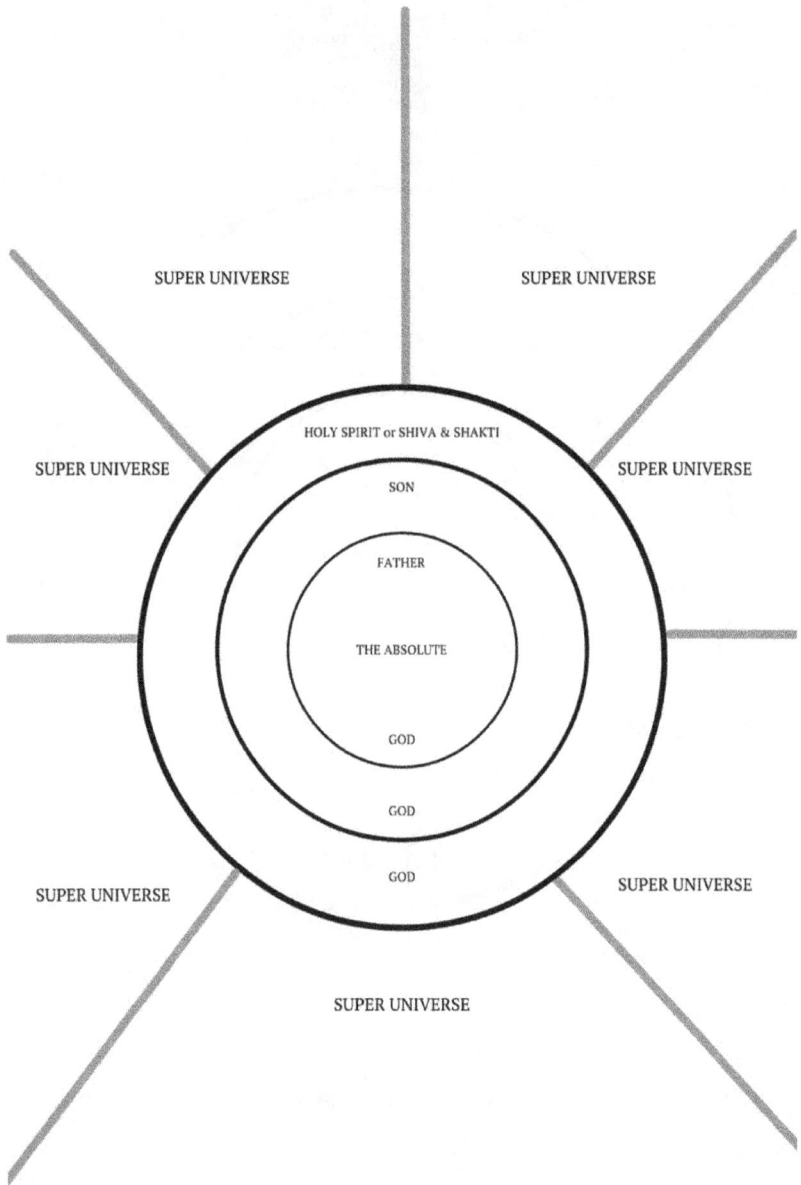

SUPER UNIVERSE

SUPER UNIVERSE

SUPER UNIVERSE

SUPER UNIVERSE

HOLY SPIRIT or SHIVA & SHAKTI

SON

FATHER

THE ABSOLUTE

GOD

GOD

GOD

SUPER UNIVERSE

SUPER UNIVERSE

SUPER UNIVERSE

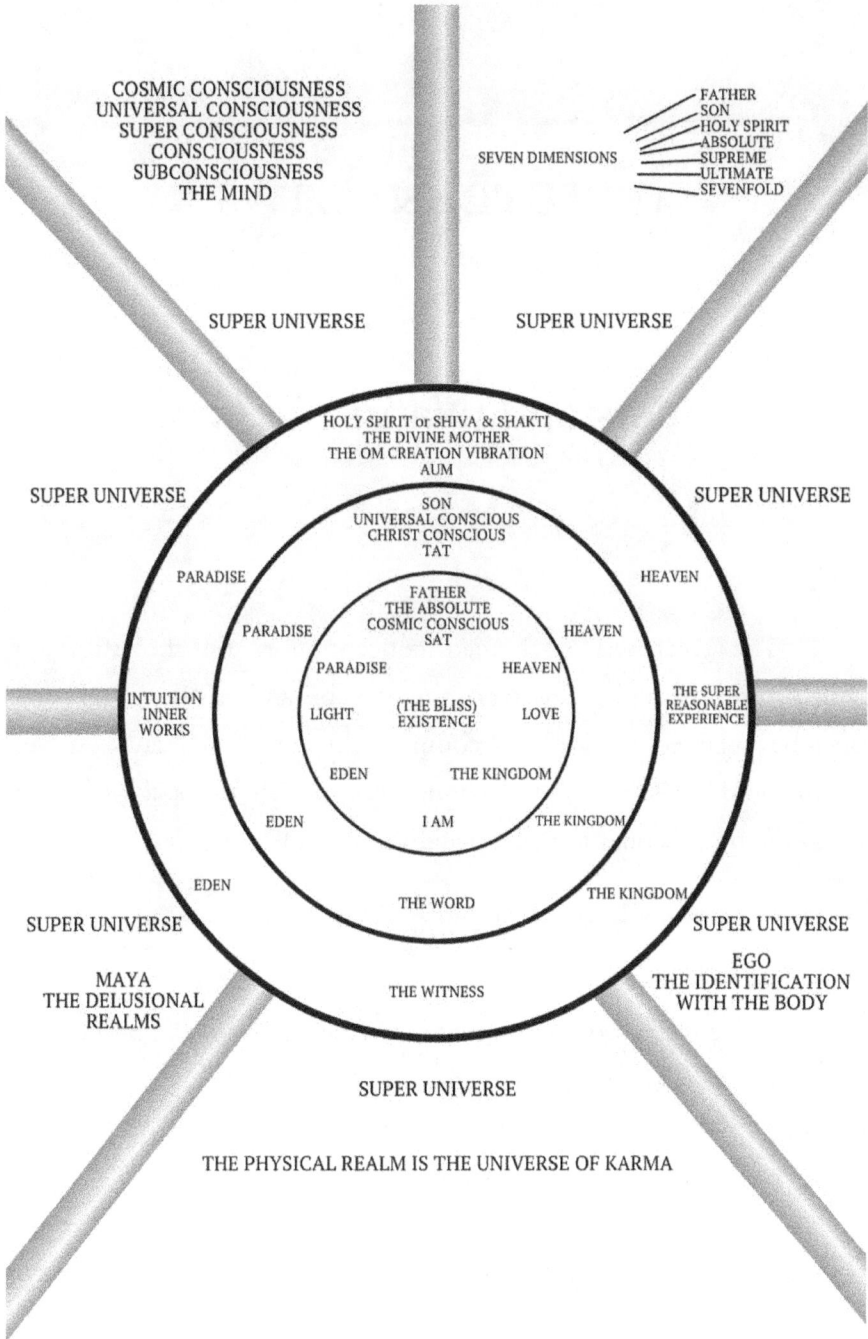

COSMIC CONSCIOUSNESS
UNIVERSAL CONSCIOUSNESS
SUPER CONSCIOUSNESS
CONSCIOUSNESS
SUBCONSCIOUSNESS
THE MIND

SEVEN DIMENSIONS

FATHER
SON
HOLY SPIRIT
ABSOLUTE
SUPREME
ULTIMATE
SEVENFOLD

SUPER UNIVERSE

SUPER UNIVERSE

SUPER UNIVERSE

SUPER UNIVERSE

HOLY SPIRIT or SHIVA & SHAKTI
THE DIVINE MOTHER
THE OM CREATION VIBRATION
AUM

SON
UNIVERSAL CONSCIOUS
CHRIST CONSCIOUS
TAT

FATHER
THE ABSOLUTE
COSMIC CONSCIOUS
SAT

PARADISE

HEAVEN

PARADISE

HEAVEN

PARADISE

HEAVEN

INTUITION
INNER
WORKS

LIGHT

(THE BLISS)
EXISTENCE

LOVE

THE SUPER
REASONABLE
EXPERIENCE

EDEN

THE KINGDOM

EDEN

I AM

THE KINGDOM

EDEN

THE KINGDOM

THE WORD

SUPER UNIVERSE

SUPER UNIVERSE

MAYA
THE DELUSIONAL
REALMS

THE WITNESS

EGO
THE IDENTIFICATION
WITH THE BODY

SUPER UNIVERSE

THE PHYSICAL REALM IS THE UNIVERSE OF KARMA

Nature & Laws

Understand (Nature & Laws)

The receptacle of human concentration, on the effort of evolving into the understanding of the universe and its nature and laws, must be enlarged in order to comprehend nature and laws and to comprehend oneself. A bowl cannot contain all the soil on Earth unless the bowl is built to contain all the soil on Earth.

What are Nature & Laws?

There is a law of nature that says God exists for the purpose of adventure and exploration, all to entertain Himself. Nature and laws are alive and spirited. Nature and laws are the key components to our soul and human journeys, adventures and explorations.

Spirit, soul and nature are some of the many personalities of existence (God). God is functional through nature and its laws. Nature, as mentioned before, is a definition of God. Understanding the universe's laws is to substantiate the way nature works. To know nature is to comprehend how to apply laws. To know nature is to be one with nature and to understand the circumstances and conditions throughout our day-to-day interactions, of our overall human journey and experience. If we are able to appreciate and comprehend nature, we could begin to exercise nature's laws in order to experience harmony with nature and its laws of our mental state to wellness.

Spirituality and science have a fundamental resemblance that is parallel to the bearings of both, and that is they are both bolstered by nature's laws and principles. Laws govern nature. Laws take you from destination to destination. Nature and laws' association in the structure of how things work throughout the human experience is precisely employed, determined and resolute through the wisdom of applying nature's laws and principles. The nature and laws on how life develops discloses the process of our past, current and future conditions.

This is what we call cause and effect. The Bible phrase rendition is sowing and reaping, which is the Hindu and Buddhist word phrase that is simply just the concept known as karma. They all possess the same meaning. Karma is a basic law of nature and a law of this lower delusional realm we are all in.

The simple fact that the evidence of our past history and life experiences unveils the principle that says "we are all a product of our life experiences" is very relevant and influenced by nature and its laws.

For instance, let's say someone experiences, as a child in particular, a discovered ability. An ability such as writing poems, or some sort of art ability, and perhaps becomes able to use this talent as a profession and is able to affect many troubled lives, in a positive and productive way. A way that would one day result in individuals who would be affected by these talents, that would one day affect the writer or person of art in a healing matter. This would be the process of the laws of nature and how the principles of nature are displayed.

Then we have some who have encountered some type of trauma of some sort and never have taken the time, or even knew to take the time, or thought it to be necessary to seek out some type of mental remedy of the matter. They would at some point in time affect another person in a traumatic way, who would also go on to harm many others.

This would also be the law of nature and the process of nature. To understand the process of nature is to possess the logical awareness of the possible success of a mental health and wellness treatment system for all, and its necessary urgent need at our present moment in time.

The Cause & Effects of Nature & Laws

Nature begins with the absolute, cosmic conscious state and dimension, where light and the laws within the light are summoned to the universal conscious state and dimension. To be exercised into creation by the Om vibration and witness state and dimension. Existence is nature governed by laws. Nature's laws say, "what we allow ourselves to see, is what will be." The laws of nature say, "we all can become what we surround ourselves with and we can all become what we practice." These principles define the cause and effects of the laws of nature. According to nature, we are all in the midst of past, present and future surroundings, and customs and practices that all lead to our current and future results. Nature and its laws are the cause and effect of all matters of existence (God) and of the life experiences of the present, because the present reveals that we are all currently in the past and future according to the law of consciousness.

The nature of humanity's past state lingers in the form of symptoms that remain in our present mass state. It dictates the outcome that reveals the nature of our current collective dysfunctional and potentially progressive mental state of positive and negative psychological conditions—ones that have and will result at some point in either a satisfying or tumultuous consequence. According to the applied law to whatever nature presents, or humanity presents, the liability in the normalization of where we were collectively, psychologically and are currently in our mass state, society must swiftly rearrange to a new approach to how we deal with mental health. Understanding the anatomy of nature will work out our existing mentally dysfunctional circumstances.

By contemplating on universal nature and laws toward our present collective state, by applying laws of reasoning combined with vision and intuitiveness and the will to do so, the comprehension of law and nature can disentangle our present mental abnormality and sufficiently tend to the interpretation and understanding of nature. Universal laws and awareness of nature is a paramount priority one must seek to enshrine, to connect to a logical explanation of why a mental health and wellness treatment system for all would be reasonable in this moment in time.

Love

There has always been a mannerism on our planet of conventionally examining, misconceiving and practicing insufficient confined perspectives of the word love. It is a word and human experience that when misconceived will have an indefinite impression upon humanity's universal, evolutional, and exploratory growth and development. So let us delve into the concept of love to determine its association with mental soundness.

What is Love, and what are its Characteristics?

Love, as stated before, is another definition of the word God. It is one of multiple key centered natures of God. It navigates in the center of the Father as viewed on the map of God, moving outward and from the outer realms back to the center bliss, feeding bliss (the joy of the Lord) as bliss feeds love throughout existence. It is secondary to the bliss. It is omnipresent.

Though bliss and love are as one, the light, which is also known as the knowledge or the truth, dwells in the midst of the bliss along with love. Love is why humanity exists. One of the most critical segments of the definition of love is that love is all the nourishments of life. Love is an action. It is an action that creates emotional consequences, it is the actions of all the nourishments of life. Anything that nourishes life is an action of love, and the action itself is love.

In the Bible, love is described in I Corinthians 13:4–7 as saying, "Love suffers long and is kind; Love does not envy; Love does not parade itself, is not puffed up; does not behave rudely, does not seek its own, is not provoked, thinks no evil; does not rejoice in iniquity, but rejoices in the truth; bears all things, believes all things, hopes all things, endures all things." As said, true love really never fails.

In the past and throughout pop culture, we have heard some utter words such as "love sucks" or "love stinks." The word love is prevailingly misunderstood and misinterpreted. Most humans either do not know the definition of love, or possess a restricted level of understanding the definition of love. It is realized that many have disoriented egos that restrict their cognizance of love. The witness and evidence, mentioned in the prior demonstration, from the chapter: Awaken to the Idea of a Solution; under the topic: Evidence that Witness our Mass Mental Paralysis, that confirms this restricted awareness of love is also evident in the behavioral appearance of humanity, prevalent throughout social media. The word love is a diluted adoration—it is faulted for our woes as a customarily diluted human practice on our planet. Though at the same time, it has been adored.

Nevertheless, it has yet to become a sufficiently established procedure. The concept of love demands and requires a balanced measure of understanding in order to have a functional, mentally balanced, competent and civilized society. Love is the identity and center of ourselves. It is also the mechanism that is the catalyst of understanding oneself. Love must be applied to oneself. There is no efficiency in loving others without knowing how to love oneself. The application of proficient proportionate love employed by humanity bestows the ability to obtain empathy, compassion, and kindness to administer into society. The available apprehension of love is proportionate to each and every human being. The more you understand the subject of love, the more influence it will have on your mental and psychological state, which may ultimately alter one's behavior, in an impactful, productive, reasonable and sane condition.

Mental anxieties, depression and stress release bad toxins throughout the body that ultimately lead to sickness, diseases and death. The effect of love, which installs a peace of mind and mental balance, releases good toxins throughout the body that generate the outcome of good health and longevity. The effect of true love will result in the success of nourishing one's mental health.

A wholesome understanding of love allows you to have the capacity to be able to discern the elemental aspects of love. True love is an authoritative force that will improve one's self-confidence. It will grant you the capability and insight to recognize whether you are conducting yourself in an adequate and balanced love. This will also help you, should you possess an interest in assessing and determine if someone, such as a spouse or friend, knows love, or how to love, or wants to be loved. The measure of love that is understood will determine and solve the interest in all matters, including the implementations of love within a mental health and wellness treatment system, for all.

Spirit & Soul

What is the Spirit and the Soul & How do they Behave?

The human spirit is God. It is God blasting Himself out into billions of pieces of creations to lose Himself, all but to turn around and find Himself once again, intentionally as Himself, a partner and companion. The human soul is God, and has also been blasted out into billions of pieces of creation along with the human spirit. There is a distinction between the spirit and the soul. The spirit is the characteristic of all human existential experiences. It is the absolute nature of existence—spirit is existence itself and its essence. The soul is the mental memory of existence and spirit—it is the passenger, explorer and adventurer of the spirit, and its psyche and essence.

However, through the law that determines spirit as being omnipresent, the soul as well as the spirit is resolved as omnipresent. This is so because the spirit and the soul are never disjointed. God is eternal and immortal. God is spirit and the super soul, which is eternal and immortal. Human beings (according to Genesis 1:26) are in the image and likeness of God. This means we too are eternal and immortal. The purpose of our human journey is to evolve and arrive back to the conclusion, awareness and practice of our soul's evolutional immortality. The human soul and spirit cannot be killed or destroyed.

Some in mainstream religion state that they are eager to go to heaven and live in eternity, but to put it bluntly, they don't realize that they are already living in eternity. We are all evolving back to the state and realization of who and what we are, the immortal spirit and soul. The immortal soul exhibits the knowledge that we are all time travelers, and reveals our multiple immortal experiences. Our experiences of déjà vu reveals our immortal, eternal time travels.

What is Déjà Vu?

So that you may have some clarity on the matter of what déjàvu reveals, I will amplify a bit more on other vital components of the human soul.

The human soul consists of memory and feeling. So the experience of déjà vu that says in infinite memories, "I have been here before, and I sense and feel like I have been here or encountered this particular person or circumstance before," is the occurrence that explains the human soul's infinite memories. Déjà vu is memory. Déjà vu is the soul's memory. The human spirit and soul is timeless, it has been existing, living and experiencing for an eternity.

The Nature of Attachments

As human beings, we encounter the experiences of attachments. Attachments are the fetters of passions. Desires and likes are from the soul's memories of moments. The things undesired and disliked are from the soul's memories as well. Likes and dislikes are shackled by the attachments to the passions of whatever likes and dislikes the soul remembers. Attachments are identified as well as the fixational, devotional, obsession and cause of habits. Likes and dislikes are generated by consciousness, which also comes in the form of memory of the soul's past, present, future, eternal, mortal and immortal states of being. Likes and dislikes are the evidence of the soul's memories and the soul's memories are the evidence of the soul's immortality. Addictions and phobias are attachments of memories of the soul, that results in the cause to the effect of one's karmic outcome of mental delusional distortions. The soul's memories occupy the explanation of why some have or are born with acrophobia (the fear of heights), or encounter and experience a strong liking to someone or something. Attachments remain with the soul throughout eternity, up until the end of its judgement and/or the attachment has been exercised out of one's psyche. This means that your attachments create who, what, and where you are and go.

Creation

Therefore, God has created you with the ability to create yourself, though at the same time this does not mean you were not created by God. This only means that, on this lower plane of the journey of life and blending back to what you are and were before, what you do is what you create, and will determine where you go. Orchestrated by God and the nature of existence, we are created to create ourselves.

Only God Exists (Who We Are)

So if God has blasted Himself out into many pieces of Himself in creation, this not only means we (all creation) are God, but this also means that we are each other in another lifetime and in another life form.

This particular phrase "we are God" must not be taken out of context. The phrase simply means that if you poke a piece of God, you have poked God. If someone encounters a pinch on the arm, you don't say, "a piece of John's arm was pinched," you say, "John was pinched."

When we do harm to each other, we do harm also to ourselves, and when we do good to one another, we do good to ourselves.

In the Bible, Jesus teaches one of the greatest laws and commandments to abide by. In Matthew 22:39, Jesus says, "you shall love your neighbor as yourself." This could be rephrased as, "you shall love your neighbor as yourself because you are your neighbor," according to the true nature and sense of the words "spirit" and "soul." Especially if there is only one consciousness that we all share, which makes us all the same spirit and soul.

The principle that says, knowing one's self empowers oneself to make able our mental balance is of truth. Tuning into the knowledge and the frequencies of the human spirit and soul could and will assign a more positive and assurable effect on our mental solidity. A mental health and wellness treatment system for all can accomplish our empowerment to know the elements of ourselves, our spirit and soul.

The Ego

Out of all the different aspects of our human makeup, the ego has been described as peculiar and complicated. It is the most important aspect of the mind to explore. To understand the dimensional dynamics of the ego could be one's game changer. So let us dissect the anatomies of the ego.

What is the Ego, and what is the importance of knowing it?

The ego is the part of the mind that identifies with the body or self, with phrases such as I, me, my and myself. There are two components of the ego: the selfless and the selfish. The selfless ego is the awareness of the higher self and the doer of all things—the universal and cosmic conscious self and perception. The selfish ego is the lower ego that identifies with the body, or the perception of the individual self, as the delusional perceived ultimate doer of all matters of the self. It is the victim and the sufferer of this human experience. Many can only grasp the ego in the context of meaning self-centeredness. However, the ego, characterized in the context of meaning self-centeredness, debilitates a thorough perspective of the word.

The ego is the main cause of dualism. Dualism is a delusion, and a perceptional standpoint and viewing of the separation between man and God. The prospect of the word ego is obligated to a view measured in the direction of understanding its totality. This means that the more we understand the ego, the more constructive the impact on one's self-awareness and mental soundness. The magnitude of attentiveness, in reference to the ego, is conducive to mental harmony and plausible to an accommodation of a raptured state.

Characteristics of the Unattended to Ego

The ego unattended to does the following. It remains dysfunctional or disconnected from spirit and the higher self. It establishes itself as the enemy of wisdom and knowledge. It is dishonest and deceptive to others and oneself. It endures and tolerates attachments to desires, pleasures and aggravations. It distorts and dilutes you from reality. It prohibits you from an evolving, multi-dimensional conscious state. It will diminish the insight of your purpose in life. It subdues you to the delusional psychological realms of being.

The unattended-to ego administers a near sighted state of mind. It is the reason why our present-day politicians lack the creative ideals, moral insight, and creative imagination to solve problems and govern. The unattended-to ego also lacks empathy: the capacity to identify with nature and others. It is the reason why we are all, through our current political climate, talking at each other instead of talking to each other, as Malcolm Gladwell enlightens us in his bestseller: *Talking to Strangers*. The ego unattended to is one of the explanations of the prevalent mental paralysis that flourishes here on earth.

Characteristics of an Attended to Ego

Now the ego attended to does the following. It allows the intuition firm detection, and the soul's functionality to flourish in order to give rise and awaken the higher self. It bestows the gift to accumulate universal knowledge and wisdom, through the exercise and the procedure of meditative self-reflection. It instills an awareness and honesty to the self (the lower ego). The attended-to ego is free from the attachments to likes and dislikes and develops tolerance. It is awakened to eternal realities and multidimensional conscious states. The attended-to ego gives one insight to one's purpose in life, and administers clear insight to one's mind and creative imagination. It has the ability to empathize with nature's circumstances and others. The attended-to ego has the potential to cure our current political, social and spiritual climate.

Attended-to ego looks like effective therapy, with multiple meditative exercises, affirmations and concentrations, like the following. Self-reflecting 2–3+ times daily, until you have reached the goal of maintaining a meditative twenty-four hour state. Kriya yoga, day in and day out. To do, to act and react to the universe and universal laws during daily duties and services. Concentrating while sitting in silence, meditating on the anatomy of the laws and principles of the universe. Using methods and practices of implementing the laws of prayer while administering the psychological devices to prosper one's practice. Psychological devices are any detailed mechanisms that may assist one's intent, purpose, goals and practices, especially attending to the ego with the intent of a mental health and wellness treatment system for all.

The Process of Evolving to the Higher Ego

As the soul evolves and consolidates to the spirit, and repeatedly exercises higher self-awareness and receives the knowledge and wisdom of spirit, the lower ego begins to take a back seat, in awe, as a fan and admirer of the newly realized super conscious higher self. It becomes unattached to pleasures and resentments and all other attachments of the human experience. The human—lower and higher ego—continues to experience pleasure and passion, just only without the attachments. It gradually increases soundness, a clear mind and a connection to reality, and you become centered and mentally balanced. In the higher states of universal and cosmic consciousness, the lower ego relinquishes its self-significance. Under universal and cosmic consciousness, the lower ego sustains its dwelling, but only as transfixed in the oneness of spirit. A famous person who I admire was on the hit TV show, The Talk, once stated, "I don't know how you could train humanity in someone, et cetera." My recommendation would be to simply and systematically exercise self-awareness and therapeutic treatment of a person's disgruntled mental state, no matter the crime or sin. Our emotions brood from the illusions, and our ego tends to assess the abnormal experiences of human matters in unnatural psychological narratives. This is why and how humanity captures the incapacitated clamorous positions of the recycled mental tyranny of the lower ego, which tends to have a normalizing effect on societies.

Nevertheless, we all make statements that are detrimental to societal progress. The higher self and ego is detected in the intent of all actions of selflessness, which is love. A therapeutic treatment system for all could show the embodiment of awareness of how the lower ego affects us all and how it could be rectified through the higher self and ego. A mental health and wellness treatment system for all can awaken our higher selves and ego.

KEYS TO OUR

WOES

Conversations

The Keys

The Product of Environment

The Effect of Oppression and Depression

The Universal Law of Influential Effects of Our Environment

Every human on our planet is embedded in the consequences of our generation's current collective psychological dysfunctional state of being. The take on this position is a universal law that is evident throughout our history and present day events and conditions. I call attention to this truth and the nature of this truthful universal law to provide some insight and an explanation on how we all become who we are, so we all can enhance the healing factors on moving forward from our abnormal environmental, psychological disharmony. We must first pay attention to the toxic psychological environment, conditions and influences. Many to this day identify with the psychological influences of past and present generations, consciously or subconsciously. The view on how we identify who and what we are, and were prior, could be considered a delusional and deceptive perspective. With that said, there is a law and truth that also affirms what you do or have done is not who or what you truly in essence are and truly were. It is what state you are and were in, at that present moment and what state of mind you were at before. Mental environmental states from the past and present play a part in how we see ourselves and partake in what we do and why we do it.

Many human beings around the world are born into dysfunctional circumstances and families with no structure. Many are brought up in mainstream, religious, indoctrinated views of themselves and the world that are mundane and plagued with falsehoods and mistaken beliefs. The outcome of such conditions establishes itself in the form of spiritual and mental fissures and obscurities that could possibly result in mental destabilizations and abuse being the operating order and development for one's journey in many forms along the way. The pervasively, seemingly settled psychological normalizations of some dysfunctional experiences are neglected and disregarded, which triggers and affects other mental impediments. For instance, education affirmed as unimportant to some politicians has a massive negative effect on those they govern, and a recurring psychological effect in conformity to political traditions. Repetitive violence and bullying experienced as a child, and then the transpiration of becoming the perpetrator, becomes complicated and common.

A human being who becomes a product of their environment comprises all of their conditions, surroundings, circumstances and experiences.

Environmental Effect of Racism

For an African-American, the circumstances and experiences would also encompass the residue and symptoms of a people subjugated, by the residue and symptoms of injustice and abuse that stems from the time of slavery. However, even well after the emancipation and up to this current time period and climate, the residue and the symptoms of the injustice of slavery persist.

Now, the sin of slavery committed on such an immense scale could and already has the effect and impact of a generational curse. This curse has been inherited, even up to this generation, on both sides of the act and the sin of slavery.

Some Psychological Effects on the Side of the Oppressor

On the side of the oppressors, the curse will resolve as the curse of the slave owners from the past to the descendants of the slave owners by the law of karma, until one breaks the curse. The result of a passed down curse from the sin of slavery will conclude in the form that subdues the ego to elements of captivity. When the ego is subdued, there is no ability to self-reflect. When there is no self-reflection, there is also no repentance (change of mind: the adjustment away from the way you once viewed the sinful act and perspective to a more truthful and mature perception and response). True repentance equals true healing results. When there is no true repentance, there is also evidence of a lack of an ability to empathize that is caused by the ego. When one lacks the ability to empathize, one tends to dehumanize the oppressed, and thus becomes immune and resistant to being attentive to the suffering of the oppressed and others. This also leads to living in delusional effects of repeated, monotonous bondage to one's own misfortunes. Misfortunes such as not only the inability to recognize inequality, but also depriving one's self of the capacity to recognize the eventual personal effects of inequality.

One of the curses of those who exercise oppression on others, looks like an inheritance of depression for themselves, in many forms.

The symptoms of the descendants of those who have practiced slave ownership share a generational curse that would also expose itself in the delusional perception and practice of the superiority complex. The superiority complex is inherited through a debilitated ego. It is like a false observation that views a scientist as being a superior human being to an infant child, rather than just understanding that the scientist is only more knowledgeable than the infant child. The problem lies within the egotistical identification of self that lures a deranged practice of individualism. The superiority complex opens the doors to the symptoms of being socially deprived. Socially deprived in the sense of seeing yourself as entitled, privileged, elite and always in the right, and the rest of the world—other nations, races and ethnicities—as wrong. Therefore, they tend to regard themselves and their nation, race or ethnicities as superior to others, just as some highly educated and opulent out-of-touch person would behave. For that reason, they never endeavor to learn or understand the importance of equality for other cultures, nations, races and ethnicities. So the response to others, may result in the dehumanization of their fellow human beings. If there is no tending to such a subdued ego, the consequences of a disdainful delusional generation that is initiated from a previous oppressive generation's conclusion will always emerge in the devastation of the soul's psychological and dissolving spiritual descent. This is what we see unfolding in today's societies.

Some Psychological Effects on the Side of the Oppressed

On the side of the oppressed, there is also the curse and symptoms of slavery and some beyond that has an impression on our historical and present-day events and conditions. The generational curse and symptoms of the oppressed from the time of slavery to the current moment also encounters the impediments of the subdued and unattended-to ego. The captivity of the ego affects generations of the oppressed in the form of community depression and individual depression. Depression affects us all in different ways. Many who are dealing with depression that has an association with oppression can and do develop behavioral proclivities that oppress others, who may in turn eventually inherit depression themselves. The unattended-to and captive ego can be restricted from the abilities to identify the inability to implement universal laws of truth that will accommodate adequate relief from depression and oppression. So with that said, until there is a cohesive breakthrough on the insight of the universal natural law of the ego that yields truth, there resumes a repeated cycle and reciprocation of oppression and depression, and vice versa. Especially when the individuals and communities are beguiled into mainstream religious, half truthful, conditional interpretations and fabrications. In today's psychology and psychiatry, we have an increased measure of understanding of the details of depression. That said, there are many professionals who choose to be unconcerned with or oblivious to the serious everyday encounters of somberness and depression. Therefore, the nature and outcome of the symptoms and residue of such daily encounters elongates and nurtures individual, community and societal depression.

Psychological Conditions & Consequences of the Bully Complex

Many speak out and oppose bullying in today's climate, but when addressed inefficiently, the mentally debilitating practice endorses sustainable oppression and depression.

The tolerance of bullying dwells in systematic social symptoms from the past up to this day. It resembles social and economic inequality for black and brown communities, and even for poor whites in the richest country on our planet. To tolerate some selective bullying is to defeat the whole purpose of contesting bullying. What you allow to dwell in your nest stays in your nest. That is a universal law. If a human being has a terminal disease or a life-altering medical condition that will or will not terminate one's life, and is unable to receive medical assistance due to not being able to pay or afford medical insurance, this would be considered bullying, blasphemous and an outright malicious atrocity.

The Situation We are In

There is a vivified hopelessness in those who experience depression. If it's by way of oppression, it will in some way reclaim those who oppress others. According to the World Health Organization (WHO) that as of 2017, 300 million people around the world have depression and also based on one of the most recent depression statistics, the American Academy of Pediatrics mentioned that 60% of children and adolescents with depression are not getting any type of treatment. In 2017, the National Institute of Mental Health stated that, in a given year, major depressive disorder affects 17.3 million American adults, or about 7.1% of the U.S. population age 18 and older. Can you imagine how many others have depression not included in those statistics, and the trickle-down effect on others from those who suffer from any sort of depression? There is said to be about forty million people in America who are dealing with chronic or clinical depression, and one out of four or five children are dealing with depression as well. Though surely you could simply see all around you, the widespread numbers are apparently much more, perhaps in the hundreds of millions or more. Many are undetected and undiagnosed. Many are dealing with depression, but have yet to identify depression within oneself. Depression is all around our world. To have allowed matters of our collective mental paradox to vigorously thrive for as long as we collectively have says a lot about all of us (humanity).

In order to rehabilitate and empower oneself to a balanced mental state, one must reevaluate one's own mental status. An awareness, acknowledgment and explanation would be essential to the restorative process.

Humanity has been recycling its infected virus of oppression and depression throughout recorded history, with the veil of the delusional standardized distorted reality of normalizing such practices and state of being.

An Environmental Guarantee Resolve for Social Movements

The bar has been set low for man for centuries. The Me Too and Times Up movements have been long overdue. This is the moment we all contribute our self-reflective inner work perspectives to the cause and effect (karma) of change.

The way men interact with women must be reevaluated in every household. Every aspect of how men have bullied women must be addressed. Men are going to need the consistent and persistent voice of women.

For men who see these movements as a threat of some sort, these movements are also your blessing in disguise. All oppression and depression through these movements is now in the opportunistic scope of decline.

These two movements must be guided by justice only, and not injustice, because the act of injustice will only set back any progress of these movements and other measures of inequality. The two movements require by nature, universal law and what we call God, the position of addressing all oppression and depression in order to subsist and sustain change. The state of our current, collective, spiritual, mental and psychological disposition shines light on our behavior, everyone of us (humanity), as being the product of our environment. A mental health and wellness treatment system for all can sow and harvest, products of environments of equanimity and rapture, that will one day solidify favorable and reasonably just resolutions to movements such as Times Up, Me Too and beyond.

The End of the System of Belief

The Beginning of the System of Perception

Belief

Belief: trust or confidence, a firm opinion, to assume.

Belief has been a significant eminent component within the principles of mainstream religion. However, within the laws and nature of spiritual truths, belief can be the beginning law that evolves one into faith and the measures of faith.

Faith & Conviction

Faith is conviction. Conviction is sureness, through the seeing or viewing from perceptions of matters of the human experience. Faith evolves one up to the ranks of universal and cosmic consciousness.

Perception in Comparison to Belief

Belief also has its discrepancies and weaknesses caused by the ego, due to the facts and evidence of truth that one can believe in anything, even delusions and falsehoods. Many in mainstream religions suffer the incapacitation of being complacent with only the rank and measures of belief. The nature of complacency in belief only, without the evolutional measures of faith, equates to the natural result of delusion and falsehoods. Faith, without the intuitive possessing of truth perspectives (the intuitional inner works, the Witness, the Holy Spirit), may intertwine one with delusion. Delusional belief that is caused by the ego usually will consciously or unconsciously justify our broken perspectives to sustain whatever particular delusional preference or aversion. For instance, one may hold onto the idea that the earth is flat instead of round, even though the scientific discovery that the earth is round has been well established and confirmed. The delusional ego may simply tune out any of science and nature's highly reasonable evidence that could pervasively be encountered throughout the human experience.

Within the fragilities of this tool called belief, we have all used this word fraudulently, as well as the multitudes in mainstream religions. We have all been in acceptance of our world's stagnation in systematic practices of distorted delusional beliefs while verbalizing the word "faith." We should all know the difference between the two, and that belief is not faith.

Perception

Perception: 1) The ability of perceiving. 2) Intuitive recognition of truth. 3) Aesthetic quality of awareness, consciousness, realization, et cetera.

The difference between intuitional perception and just belief is that the former is more of an experienced noticing of the realization of truth in the viewing of ecstatic recognized intelligence. Perception can also encounter delusional features when the ego and belief combines and overwhelms perception. With the ego alone, one can experience the components of perceptional delusions. Belief can have the attributes of ignorance that unveil the aspects of the ego that displays pride, vanity and the results of fake and false proof, as well as some discoveries of truth. When belief is the only measure of acceptability in one's spiritual voyage, one's spiritual growth and evolutional standing will eventually experience crippling and stagnant results. Within such spiritual stagnation comes the state of symptoms and manifestations of mental disorders and delusions (maya).

This is also why belief mustn't be the only standardized and normalized acceptable method to obtain the empowerments of intelligence and truth.

The ability of perceiving by way of intuitive recognition, as well as the enduring and experiencing of intelligence and truths, that settles in rational perception and perspectives, is now the focal point of our approach to the connection of our rational perceptions. This type of perception has a certainty from the components that one experiences. This perception is defined as conviction.

The high measures of perception are the ultimate goal and operational procedure to self-awareness. When one endures others in these days describing their beliefs, it is more likely to be taken lightly than to be taken as practical, as the truth or fact. However, when one endures others describing perceptional intuitive facts and intelligence with the true meaning and experience of the word faith, one begins to receive an experience in detailed, intuitive, rational facts and intelligence.

Perceptional delusions are rooted in the ego by ignorance and the attachments in the passions of likes and dislikes. With an intuitive and intelligent perception of rational facts and the approach of "humbleness" toward the amassment of the facts, the delusional perceptions have no power.

So we must now begin to seek out the higher magnitudes of perceptions in order to deal with our everyday mental distortions. Perceptions in detailed description, through the experience of a detailed "ecstatic feeling" of factual perception, is equated to humble empowerments to the realization of one's true higher self. The ecstatic feeling of factual perception that I'm describing is that "ah ha" moment that we all experience when we have encountered that moment of factual feeling of a realized result.

This account of perception I am describing to you is also the identification of the true sense of the words faith and conviction. Here is one of the biblical descriptions of the word faith.

It states in Hebrews 11:1, "Now faith is the substance of things hoped for, the evidence of things not seen."

So the word evidence is used here. If it is an evidence of things not seen, then the proof and evidence have a functional component to its meaning and experience. The word evidence is defined as an available fact that determines truth and validity. Evidence must be perceptionally and functionally *experienced in regards to faith and belief does not.

Law of Faith

The Bible characterizes faith as being the evidence of things not seen. This means the evidence can be accumulated beyond the foundations of the external physical senses, such as the eyes and the carnal third dimensional intellectual gathering.

There are universal principles that must be applied in order to acquire an intuitive perception, or the true experience of the word faith. Here are a few. The first law is humbleness: you must be childlike minded in curiosity and eager to learn. Second, you must develop a passion and devotion to a lifestyle to this sort of perception. Third, you must always understand that no human being can ultimately supply you with the intuitive perception as your true higher self (God) can.

Perceptional Success

However, our world demonstrates an urgent call for humanity to rid ourselves from the dysfunction and complacent paralysis, of not advancing beyond the infant stages of belief. What we are all experiencing is the results of the diluted symptoms from belief. Just take a look, the proof is all around us all. Many are not able to determine the difference between real news and fake news.

We must begin to reform the way we acquire perceptional facts that determine truth. We can achieve this through meditative intuitive concentration, discriminating insight, and self-reflection processing. A mental health and wellness treatment system for all compels the outcome of perceptional success.

Reflect on Solutions

Ideals & Thoughts

Understanding Who We are in Order to See Where We Need to Go

The clarifications of the five discourses—God, Nature & Laws, Love, Spirit & Soul, and Ego—will certainly govern our current predicament and societal framework, to assurable resolutions. These subjects clarified will ultimately result in self-awareness, and the awareness of our purpose. How can humanity respond sufficiently to matters of self if there are limits to the perceptions and understanding of self? If you can see what is before you, you could then begin to interact and correlate with what you are then able to see.

Existence (God) has a persona that is mental, memorial, intuitive, consciousness (Spirit & Soul), that is governed by its way of working. Its essential characteristics and principles (Nature & Laws) are in the actions of nourishing itself (Love) by way of informing us of the

I (the Ego) to awaken our higher "I am" self. We are the five discourses one describes, waiting to be recognized within ourselves.

Knowing this to be so, we can begin to reflect on solutions and recite a few possible therapeutic propositions for a mental health and wellness treatment for all systemic success, and then a prioritized societal system.

Mental distortions are caused by maya. Maya is the physical third dimensional realm all of humanity experiences through the aspects of the ego (the identification of the body and the senses). This realm that we call maya is the realm of delusion. Maya is the lower delusion realm that is also created by ourselves. The original realms before maya are the natural realms of ourselves, the realms that are essential and also produce maya, which are known as the realms of paradise. The original realms of paradise create the delusional realms called maya. As God blasts Himself out into creation to lose Himself, all but to find Himself. For the purpose of exploration, adventure and entertaining Himself. Since God alone exists, the trust and confidence of viewing ourselves as individuals are part of the delusion.

The goal of humanity is to discover self-awareness within the original essential realms. To abide in the essential realms of Nirvana (Paradise) is to acquire the mental wherewithal of what I call the faculties of connecting the dots. Connecting the dots is to accumulate the insight and the capacity to apply discrimination (to make and see a distinction) to circumstances and principles, and administer adequate universal laws and methods suitable to all circumstances and states of being, mentally and physically.

58

Reflections & Thoughts

So a remedial operation aimed at nurturing the abilities of concentration and meditation would be a therapeutic focal point of such a system.

Each person's therapy should be precisely accommodated to one's personal diagnosis or therapeutic recommendation.

Each person's remedial need should perhaps have a measure of their religious procedures, or if they are not religious, perhaps just the scientific elements of therapy. Possibly we could initiate one-on-one routine sessions with psychotherapists. Perhaps scheduled group therapy of all sorts, self-help, self-reflection, concentrations and meditations, breathing technique meetings, meditative sound programing, physical yoga practices, et cetera. Therapist of all sorts should have mandatory psychoanalysis treatments and psychotherapy, as well. Such a system should perhaps have a weekly analysis and adjustment toward the goal of its effectiveness and evolution. For instance, after some time, maybe such a system could have a systematic review that could advance the need to implement many different types of scientific dietary treatment, as well.

Administrative qualifications to operate a mental health and wellness treatment system, for all, surgically, should also obtain some kind of weekly or monthly analysis and up to date briefings. All configurations of therapy should be disclosed and accessible to all. Every child, every adult, from the president to the sanitation worker and maidservant, and especially the entire branches of governance, beginning with Congress, women and men. A thorough mental wellness-first societal system would be essentially orchestrated and utilized, according to a committee of competent psychologists, neuroscientists, psychiatrists, sociologist, influential teachers and gurus of all sorts and from all religions and religious sects or denominations. A commission who would orchestrate such a societal system should have mandatory mental health, wellness therapeutic treatments as well.

Society must be the first to act and initiate an advocacy for such an approach to our remedial mental wellness.

The therapy of all citizens perhaps should be determined according to the magnitude of all citizens' diagnoses and therapeutic recommendations. Perhaps a basic yearly volume of therapy for one who has a balanced, determined state of a diagnosis. One could possibly obtain the basic recommendations of once, twice or every six months or possibly somewhere on the lines of something quarterly and so forth.

The elements of an effective mental health and wellness treatment societal system for all could and should determine its detailed structures and implementations.

The Will to Choose to Act

The Process of Choice & Will

The connecting of dots in reference to the procedure and the nature of the human will to choose to act must also have a sufficient magnitude of discerning in order to possess the functionality through human psychological delusions (maya) that deprives the human will to choose to act, when there is an essential purpose or vision to act upon. Let us now dissect the nature and process of the will to choose to act.

First, let's take a look at the process and meaning of the mind, ego, and thought, and how they all affect the will to choose to act. The human mind exercises its functions on the account of thought and ego. Thought is consciousness compacting itself as the mind. Consciousness was, is, and always will be. It's infinite. Humans experience the memories of thought. Memory is consciousness. Memories are encountered through the experience of karma, reaping and sowing or cause and effect, by way of human souls' eternally acquired reciprocated interactions. An eternally acquired reciprocated interaction is engaged and realized as the soul's past, present, and future's eternal being of consciousness in states and creations.

So here is how it works. The soul consists of memories and feelings. The soul experiences memories of consciousness and thought and the feeling towards what is conscious and thought about. Through the fabric of attachments to whatever conscious choice and willpower encountered in one's karma (cause and effect, reaping and sowing), the feelings and memories of attachment to one's likes and dislikes are unveiled. However, your feelings and processing of the soul's attached memories are the causes of the paralysis of the will to choose to act.

So yes, the nature and reason of the mental paralysis of the will to choose to act is due to karma and karmic attachments. Attachments can be an emotion to a particular experience encountered, or a perspective of the past, present or future of a situation that may conclude an active or inactive passionate and attached response. Attachments can be overcome by the appropriate law of nature applicable to remedy the attachment or perspective towards the past, present or future seeds and causes of whatever attachment is encountered.

The very nature of who we are as human beings ascertains why we are made to mobilize will and choice. Our human nature is to learn, to teach, to explore and adventure, and to love and evolve. In order to accomplish this, it will also consist of the mobilization of will and choice. The deviation from our human nature always settles in distorted consequences. Our planet earth is an intelligence and communication center. The inability to willfully choose to engage in the competence of intelligence and communications provides one with a life of instabilities. To engage sufficiently with intelligence and communications, one lines up with balance and purpose.

The Paralyzed Will to Choose to Act

So now we can fast forward to our present massive state of having a lack of will to choose to act.

This massive absence of a will to choose to act springs from diminished responsibilities, as well as the absence of prioritizing, which originates from a detachment from accountability. This is all caused by a lack of self-awareness, mental distortions and broken perspectives.

At the present moment, at the core of America, there resumes a historical distraction of a somber predicament. This predicament results in nationalistic and racial complications and the deterioration of moral boundaries, which results in multiple measures of discordance. In all cases of mass shootings, we see the connections to the cause and effect of our unawareness of mental distortions, but still lack the will to choose to respond to our mass mental distortions and solve the problem of mass shootings.

Now let's explore five of nature's many detailed attributes of this massive distorted state of being mentally impaired collectively, with a lack of will to choose to respond to it and how this could be so. One, when a human being is void of a balance of principles, his or her life becomes chaotic and disorderly. Humanity is deficient of a balance of principles. Principles are the focal point of the survival and advancement of human existence. Two, many leaders and many religious leaders in mainstream religion systematically condition communities to distorted perspectives of the balance of principles by way of a lack of perspective themselves. Three, when delusional distorted perspectives are conventionally conditioned traditionally, our collective consequence inevitably becomes mentally tumultuous. Depression is a practiced paralysis that distorts perspectives and paralyzes one's will to choose to act. The universal principle that states,

"What you practice is what you become, and what you surround yourself with is what you become" begins to result as so. Four, because we have a lack of mental balance in our engagements in choosing authoritative and leadership positions, we allow ourselves to be led by leaders who are corrupt and mentally unstable, and therefore they lack ideas and hope in basically every institution, so we therefore become hopeless. Five, we have to recognize that we are all accountable to our collective impaired mentally distorted state. We are so caught up within ourselves and our own families that we have yet to realize that we are all responsible and have a contribution to each other and the healing of our world, and we must all contribute to our world's mental healing. If we do nothing, we contribute to our collective demise. We are here at this time and in this world to play a part in our current predicament. If it wasn't so, we would not be here in this world at this moment.

These five depictions that explore some causes of our psychological present state of mental dysfunctional paralysis also include the shortcomings of our lack of effort to notice our collective mental inadequacies. To implement a collective structure of a mental health and wellness therapeutic system, we can perhaps assure societal improvement from our mass paralyzed will to choose to act.

The faculties that allow us to detect humanity's purgatorial dilemma are critical to our development. By universal and scientific law, one cannot willfully choose to act and respond to matters of life that one cannot sense, perceive and detect. In other words, as mentioned before, how can you respond to something you're unable to see in the first place?

Our Position on Therapy

Every attempt humanity has made in regards to making our next steps in its evolution must be in reverence to our gratitude toward our view of expanded ideas. New and broadening ideals and perspectives, such as a mental health and wellness treatment system for all, are essential to the nature of humanity's evolutional rise.

I recently viewed and observed a commercial ad with Olympic swimming champion Michael Phelps that promoted therapy and slightly promoted a destigmatization of mental therapy. This is only so because we still disparage therapy and any notion of mental therapy, as though we are all doing just fine. It is imperative for a victim who has encountered criminal wrongdoing of any sort to receive mental therapy. It is critical for those who carry out criminal and wrongdoings, or victimize others in some way, to receive mental therapy. Those on the receiving end of bullying and verbal abuse should subscribe to mental therapy, in order to make sure seeds of mental discretions are not mentally implanted, voluntarily or involuntarily. If you have experienced or watched a commonly regarded news report of any sort of human suffering, therapeutic processing should be relevant. Humanity's evolutional growth in the science of mental therapeutic understanding should be valued, respected and not shamed. It is our assurance to a road of sanity and should be systematically assembled for a well-needed world of societal healing.

The will to choose to act on the implementation of assembling a societal mental health and wellness therapeutic treatment system for all is indispensable to the achievement of world peace. Such would be a restoration from our current massive mentally dysfunctional paralysis to all that we truly are, and all that we will be.

Choices

By nature, if we do not act or accumulate the will to choose to act, we all will persist in a high percentage chance of even more encountered world havoc. Rather, it is in the form of a civil or nuclear war, or a disease outbreak of any type, like the coronavirus, or even an occurrence of a catastrophe that would stem from the effects of global warming. We are all playing a part in our collective mental and societal condition, whether we accept it or not. We all possess a free choice and will to exercise a contribution to the story and direction of where humanity goes, but we must first choose to manifest a will to act.

We must choose to will the act of humbleness. We all must comprehend the consequences of monumental immobility and the impact of championing a mental health and wellness therapeutic treatment system for all.

The very nature of humility allows us humans to reflect on ourselves to gather the adequate insight on the fact and nature on how humanity has dealt with our collective mental state and currently continues to handle our collective mental capacity.

We must possess the capability of administering a very reasonable and honest assessment of the way we view mental wellness in order to commission the human will to choose to champion for a societal mental health and wellness treatment system for all.

If humanity could make a joint exertion to gather the will to choose to act, by the nature of that we can overcome our current position. To triumph through a lack of will to choose to act is to realize one's true higher self that is already within one's self.

Mental Health, Wellness & Treatment of the Past & Present

Past and Present

With respect to past and present dealings pertaining to mental health, wellness, and therapy, our collective perspective and approach has been hazy in regards to humanity's collective progressive results. Our prior engagements toward research and development was somewhat lacking of knowledge, and for the most part, was also rather ludicrous and absurd. If we give ourselves a chance to look back as we reform and progress, we may look back and say as much.

Mental Health Treatments of the Past (and Asylums)

In the past, the mentally unbalanced were guinea pigs and subject to torturous experimentations. According to OpenStax College, the most common mental health treatment in the past was an exorcism often conducted by priests or other religious figures. Another was trephining, where a small hole is made in the skull in order to discharge demonic spirits from the body. Most treated in this manner died. Other practices involved executions or imprisonment of those with psychological disorders just as we do in the present. Many were left homeless and treated cruelly. By the 18th century, those with psychological disorders were placed in asylums. Asylums were the first institutions created for the purpose of housing people with psychological disorders. They were kept in windowless dungeons, beaten, and chained to beds with little to no contact with caregivers.

In the 19th century, Dorothea Dix led reform and more humane treatment efforts of the indigent insane, and was an advocate for creating the first American mental asylum. Despite reform efforts, typical asylums were filthy, distributed very little treatment, and kept people for decades. At Willard Psychiatric Center in upstate New York, patients were submerged in cold baths for long periods of time. Electroshock treatments often broke patients' backs.

Renee Fabian, a Los Angeles based journalist and editor, wrote the July 31, 2017 article, The History of Inhumane Mental Health Treatments, which states that at the dawn of the asylum era in the mid-1700s marked a period of some of the most inhumane mental health treatments.

Journalist Nellie Bly captured firsthand when she went undercover at Blackwell's Island Insane Asylum in New York in 1887. She was not only committed without much of an examination to determine her sanity, but Nellie Bly's conditions were harsh, cruel, and inhumane.

Many have weaponized the notion of mental instabilities upon others, in order to incriminate perhaps a family member, spouse, or an enemy in order to have them committed to past institutions of torture and experimentations. This is partially why some of the stigmatizations from past societies, with regard to mental instabilities and therapy, have been prevalently conditional, even up to these days, and have stood the test of time.

Only what we are experiencing today, in the 21st century, has there been a bit more improvement, of some extreme components, over prior societies. For instance, in today's scientific vantage, we are much more advanced than our past scientific positions. With a more broadened scientific observation, comes the dignity and respect to the very subject of mental health in today's societies, compared to the past.

The past societies were without the dynamics of social media, search engines, and internet access. Network systems of the past were not as competent as today's internet. Past societies were not as able as today's societies when it comes to the exchanging of information and having a more tangible and rapid satisfiable outcome from the exchanged information as we enjoy today. An in-depth collective awareness of our mental state today may show more comprehension on the importance of our collective equanimity.

The Affect from Religion & Science

Past and present societies have had, through the inadequacies of the knowledge of spiritual science, limited interpretations of their religions, along with many in the past and present who have practiced their limited intellectual scientific analysis. The proof of this perspective lies and remains in our response up to the present era, toward mental health and wellness therapy.

Many mainstream religions were viewed by the populations of the past and partially societies of the present as the gatekeepers or the only owners of spirituality or spiritual science. Our past and present societal viewing of such a false perspective impels our humanity with the collective mental conflicts we face today. This false impression has the equivalent of some earthly government as the owner of the very air we all breathe.

Now in contrast to the rational assessment of that, we all witness the conclusions in today's misfortunes, through the uncertainty and skepticism and contradictions between science, religion and societies. We have witnessed the creation of multiple weapons of mass destruction that could annihilate us all. We have witnessed faulty science aimed at our poisonous food and cosmetic supply system. We witness many scientific ingenuities that have a devastating impact on our environmental conditions. We have religions that interpret their religion as being the only way to truth and salvation. We have religions that have practiced the perceptional conditions of carnal prosperity and greed. We all witnessed the widespread sexual misconduct and lasciviousness that has plagued religion up to this present era.

Our past religious and scientific viewing and conditions to some measures has shaped the destination of our present collective mental positions. Just as today's actions, of reciprocating yesterday's actions, can also match the same actions conducted tomorrow. The skepticism and contradictions instrumental to the witnessing of some matters and conditions of science and religion in humane societies has everything to do with the inadequacies of wisdom and knowledge and a lack of application of past and present societal prioritizations of true spiritual science.

Today's society has been oblivious to the urgency for a mental health and wellness treatment system for all, as a societal priority. Without a wellness system for all, mental conflicts will be the status quo.

The Present

So up to the current moment, we can see some continuations from the past. On many measures, in the form of the stigmatizations from past societies and also in the concept of punishment.

Punishment

Let's take a look at the concept of punishment. For instance, the concept of punishment should have a universally lawful discriminatory reassessment on the applicable approach in all procedures of justice and reformatory practice and implementations in order to correct the routine sinister and demoniac attributes of human punishment. When humans exercise punishment, it is normally distributed from the emotion of anger and ego with the intention of revenge, even when the intention of revenge is hidden within one's ego, which is one of the main characteristics of the ego. Remember, the ego can hide one's true intention. This is why we are to practice meditative self-reflection in order to uncover whatever matters that is hidden and veiled within. The initiation of revenge is not an appropriate justice.

Disciplinary practices are reasonable for a functional society. Though when punishment is delegated to a person or a situation without mental equanimity and tolerance, the outcome normally equates to an injustice. Rather, the situation is on a small or broad spectrum. The objective of employing some sort of disciplinary implementation on a person or circumstance in a society is to manufacture a rehabilitating visible effect to a mishap within a society. Sometimes discipline can be falsely perceived and received like an unjust punishment.

The component that is distinguished between real discipline and an unjust punishment is the rehabilitating reconciliatory component. An unjust punishment does not show the rehabilitating and reconcilement components. Therefore, an unjust punishment may affect a society with spiritual deprivation, societal depression, social dysfunctions, political gridlock and economical strains. Morally just and real discipline will show rehabilitating and reconcilement components and have an evolutional and productive impact on a society as a whole: spiritually, mentally, socially, politically and economically. Punishment in our societies has a sinister and mentally harmful influence on our past, present and future societies, and so punishment must be discouraged and rejected. A nation of an evolving civilization, exercising a successful approach of reconcilement instead of punishment, is legitimately on the right track to civility and progress.

Incarceration Institutions

We can take a look at our current incarceration institutions. Just as we have conducted ourselves with such matters in the past, we continue to struggle with monotonous methods of the past. Warehousing human beings with mental instabilities who have disclosed either a mild or severe case of mental malfunctions, in lockup warehouses and torturous facilities with very little to no rehabilitation taking place. Wherein the present time, in many cases, we observe daily savage violence and race riots, gang activities, sexual assaults and environments that are ripe for learning the practice of malice. Many incarceration institutions are kill-or-be-killed environments, where the killer is more accountable than the people and government who have placed him or her in such an environment.

Lockup warehouses are known as penitentiaries or prisons, which are presumed to be the installations to which humanity consigns the mentally unbalanced, in order to apply reformatory treatment for rehabilitation. Though this is not the bottom line, in most cases. In most penitentiaries they approach the responsibility of therapy and treatment with the solution of medicated drugs as their primary means and counter measure of restorative therapy. Within the most absurd part of the establishment of today's penitentiary institutions, therapeutic treatment must be requested by an inmate or the mentally unbalanced in order to be received. In most cases, many have absolutely no clue or awareness of their mental status to make such a request. In most cases, many state and federal governments irresponsibly refuse to prioritize the funding of mental health and therapeutic treatment for all prisoners in prisons, as though such treatment is not obviously and undeniably a necessity.

The American concept of life in prison with or without parole, with very little to no rehabilitating measures, is one of the sinister enactments that exposes and prolongs society's collective mental contingencies. Any societal practice that has a conflicting result or objective would be counterproductive to a mental health and wellness treatment system for all, and the collective intentional aim to the progression and advancement of a civilization. Many of today's societal structures play a part in national and international misdeeds and disturbances. Every sinful transgression society allows tends to thrive within a trickle-down effect back to the society, which affects the mental wellness of societies as a whole. The sentencing of life in prison should be influenced according to one's rehabilitating progress and status. Some may need rehabilitation for life, and some may not. Systemic inequality and societal deterioration must be met with systemic compensation. Like the restorative seed to mental abnormalities must be met with the systemic apparatus that is advocated for, known as a mental health and wellness treatment system for all. The collective and individual ego is the only matter that stands in our way.

Many state and federal government officials view the indication of funding mental health and therapeutic treatment, for all prisoners and even for the availability of all law abiding citizens, as obsolete. This is also a mental discrepancy in itself. The "let's do nothing" approach is a mental discrepancy as well. A reasonable prioritization of such a well needed policy to fund mental health therapeutic treatments for all has everything to do with the people. The people must use their voices to endorse a mental health care system for all.

The word penitentiary comes from the Latin word penilencia (penance). The word penance or penitent means to be repentant. To be repentant means to develop a change of mind in the direction of truth, correction and reconcilement. The word penitentiary also means reformatory treatment.

Today's societies are accustomed to the repetition of practicing the denial and disregard of real reformation treatment as an approach to true justice. Today's citizens have yet to see and sense the urgency and obligation of carrying out a mental health and wellness therapeutic treatment system for all. Today's societies fail to understand that what we allow to flourish in seemingly small nooks of our societies will eventually plague and infect the larger and/or all parts of communities. Does anyone care?

In many, if not all of today's penitentiaries in the United States of America, correctional officers are not given the appropriate or sufficient mental health evaluations and therapeutic treatments, while working in such a hostile and stressful environmental condition. Within most cases, if not all, the climates are of low morale. Some correctional officers go to work in these institutions for the excitement of chaos. In the form of creating some sort of race riot, or in the form of some kind of retaliation on an inmate, in order to make a name for him- or herself among other correctional officers. Does anyone care?

Today's societies fail to recognize that no effective penitentiaries are a reflection of today's societies, and that this will have an effect on law abiding citizens in many ways. Does anyone care?

Today's societies allow supremacy of a race over others to dwell among us, just as it was permitted on the days of Hitler in that particular society of the past. As though the mental discrepancy of the superiority complex were not a prior pivotal lesson of the past for humanity to learn from. Does anyone care?

With a mental health and wellness treatment system for all, placed in action over time, there will be no need for mass incarceration for prisoners that we see in today's society.

Social Media and the Internet

In our present societies, social media and the internet have exposed an imperative urgency to implement mental health and wellness therapeutic treatment for all. Every day we witness many mental turbulent breakdowns of millions of groups through internet trolls who exercise their mental malfunctions and instabilities to inflict psychological harm on their fellow human beings. Social media clearly gives us the insight on how widespread the impact of mentally unstable individuals is without any societal solution to identify, confront, treat and rectify their behaviors. Mental discordance can be detected in many corners of the internet.

Human beings yearn to be loved and accepted. Many of today's societies are attached to the urge of being loved and accepted by others online. The attachment to the longing of being loved and accepted on social media has in many cases resulted in a catalyst for mental instabilities for many in today's societies. For instance, many little girls and even adult women acquire a false sense of self-worth through imagery and many other means. Male chauvinism plays a major role in the means of many of women's mental disparities, from the past and the present societies as well. These mental discrepancies are identified through the emphasized mentally distraught comments and depictions that are expressed daily on social media.

Many of our most critical institutions in today's societies disclose low-grade standards for their employees' behavior on social media on what would normally be considered not mentally suitable as a reasonable measure of morale and professionalism. When our most critical institutions divulge low-grade mental standards of morale and professionalism, the trickle-down effect tends to plague all other institutions with the same and even more of the enhanced and heinous conditions.

The News Media

In today's society, when a tragic and horrific incident occurs, we collectively and procedurally allow unstable sources to mentally galvanize our collective perspective on the unfortunate occurrence.

Let's say, for instance, a mass shooting takes place. The first institutional fomenter to rouse our collective mental state would be news media sources almost simultaneously with social media sources. Now we know social media sources are numerous when it comes to unstable sources mentally galvanizing collective perspectives. However, the institution of the news media tends to galvanize the mental state of the masses in many fabrics of content, in some reports that phrases words in biased ways in order to shape perspectives and opinions of its audience.

There is also a normalized practice that reporters use in order to stir up mental states and perspectives of their viewers, and that is by interviewing individuals who are mentally distraught and under duress. Usually a victim, or someone close to the victim. The low-grade mental standards of the institutional media's practice of recording and broadcasting such individuals captures the mentally unstable and consequential outcomes that hinder the mental stability of our collective societies.

Media institutions have a routine practice of orchestrating broadcastings with the institutions of law enforcement, and has allowed sheriffs and other law enforcement officials during live press conferences in many cases to demonstrate and transmit mentally distraught energies. They will use energy in phrases like the words "coward" or "monster"—words that are used in today's society to psychologically dehumanize the human being. Once you have dehumanized the human being, psychologically you could begin to respond as though she or he were not a human being, which will always resort in an unjust unraveling.

Closure and Justice

The word closure is another word used by law enforcement and others that is often used out of context, and concludes unjust consequences for any and all concerned. True justice allows an injustice the fortune of an outcome of true closure. Real closure is an absolute inner mental processing of truth first that ultimately result in mental balance, righteousness and justice. Real closure does not look like the repudiation of mental therapeutic care for victims and perpetrators of unjust encounters, no matter what form or type of injustice encountered. Real closure does not look like the demonic practice of retribution. Real closure is the evidence of applied curing and reconciliation of any and all unjust circumstances and conditions. Real closure looks like a government's effective response to systemic inequality.

Today's societies often practice the word closure with measures of misleading reasoning that desecrate the laws of nature, and fundamentally interpose harmful mass mental disorderly karmic effects.

There was an incident where a law enforcement officer, from the Newman Police Department in Modesto, California, lost his life by a gang member who was allegedly an illegal immigrant. The officers who have worked closely with the officer, who had lost his life, were clearly nauseous, as one of the officers stated himself. Those officials should have been handled with the vigilance and therapeutic care and the respect that they deserved before the press conference. Instead, they were positioned too soon and almost immediately before the media cameras in a press conference that resulted in a publicized mourning session that may have aroused some viewers in mentally dysfunctional ways.

These types of press conferences take place quite often. They affect millions of viewers who are consistently dealing with PTSD (post-traumatic stress disorder), and other mental conditions of some sort.

Recycled Triggers

In today's society, we tend to ignore many contradictions that recycle and enhance our collective mental dysfunctional status. In today's society's mental influences and triggers are easily accessible and are all around our daily conditions.

Many aspects of porn are attainable to those who struggle with the mental condition of sex attachments.

Alcoholic and drug addictions in today's societies are easily attainable and still relevant. Addictions and attachments today are both subconsciously and consciously embraced. They uncover the proof of our need to establish a mental health and wellness treatment system for all.

Loneliness

How about loneliness? Loneliness in today's societies plays a significant role in today's collective mental discordance.

Some Statistics on Loneliness

In the United States (22%) and the United Kingdom (23%), more than two out of 10 adults say they always or often feel lonely, lack companionship, or feel left out or isolated, according to a 2018 survey from The Economist and the Kaiser Family Foundation (KFF).

Neil Howe a historian, economist, demographer, and a leading authority on generational trends, wrote over a dozen books and is a bestselling author. In a May 3, 2019 Forbes Magazine article, Neil Howe said, "figures like these have been ubiquitous in the press lately, within alarming statistics about loneliness now accompanied by equally alarming warnings that it's stunting our lives and outright killing us."

Social isolation triggers cellular changes that result in chronic inflammation, predisposing lonely individuals to serious physical conditions like heart disease, stroke, metastatic cancer, and Alzheimer's disease, as discovered by researchers at UCLA, in 2015.

One 2015 analysis, which collected data from 70 studies studying 3.4 million people over seven years, found that lonely individuals had a 26% higher risk of dying. This figure scaled up to 32% if they lived alone.

The Economist and KFF findings are another research out of many showing high levels of loneliness.

Loneliness is a mental conflict that is transpired from the notion and feeling of being deprived of someone, something, or some circumstance. Loneliness is the effect of an unfulfilled desire or attachment. It is also the cause of many other mental disparities and complications.

In the past and even up to this present generation, loneliness have been overlooked as a component, that played and would continue to play a significant role in today's human collective mental psyche.

In today's societies, we do not effectively administer the nourishments to loneliness and its widespread mental conflicts, which there are many.

When our journey in this life is constituted by systematic mental therapeutic treatment, our evolutional leap will begin to flourish.

What will it Look Like?

The Effect of Treatments for All

To substantiate the effects of therapeutic treatment for all, let's take a look at a reasonable, sobering proposition of what it will look like, if mental therapy became a constitutional centerpiece of our humanity.

Practically speaking, our humanity's immediate developments would reveal itself at once. Every component of our collective mental conflicts would begin to disperse in the direction of balance. Though in some measures of a mental health and wellness treatment system for all, progress may take time, for some.

The universal law that was mentioned before saying, "What you practice is what you become, and what you surround yourself with is what you become," would automatically begin to initiate its relevancy.

The implementations on multiple types of treatments of meditation would begin to have its complimentary effect on societies. Let's say for instance that the treatment of concentrated self-reflecting was the initiated utilized remedy, and the discoveries and empowerments of self-realization would have a remarkable impact. To reflect and realize oneself is to also identify with the questions and answers, the questions we all ask, that could be unveiled by means of treatment, which is to ask, "where am I currently at, where am I going, and where have I been?" These questions may lead to another set of questions, such as, "who and what was I, who or what am I, who and what will I become, or what am I becoming?" The disclosure of such questions will ultimately uncover the answers to one's purpose and blueprint, which is another question we all ask. A suitable amount of intuitiveness, reasonable self-awareness, and clear mindfullness to our purpose, individual and collective will import mental discretion and balance. Mental treatments for all will eventually affect all components of our collective spiritual awareness.

Due to mental health treatments of self-reflection and self-realization, many will begin to become not only aware of how we would treat ourselves, but also how we would treat each other. Self-realization equates to self-respect. Self-respect will open the doors to respect for each other. To come to know oneself is to become secure with oneself. When one becomes secure with oneself, the state of loneliness becomes a discontinuation. Self-reflection and realization will cure the mental discrepancies of self-hatred and insecurities that usually lead to other mental discrepancies. Self-reflection and self-realization overcome the conditions of inequality and systemic racism. Holistically, humanity's maturity standards will widen across the spectra of societies. When our ability to empathize transpires, the faculties of having ideals and visions will begin to play out in the developments of our treatments.

Social Climate

Our social gatherings will consist of an increase of intellectual substance. When we get to the point of viewing each other in higher perspectives, our actions toward each other will become more established in unity. Our day-to-day and moment-to-moment ambitions will begin to substantiate substance in wisdom and advance conscious thinking and being. Social science will have a fair chance to elevate.

Communities will begin to be more incline toward social progression and accountable for the respect and results of social diversity than in our present time. Tolerance will be proportional to the applied measures of our individual detailed treatments. Humanity will begin to sanction the acknowledgement of setbacks and paralysis of every aspect of our progress toward our evolution, from the mental disorder and delusions (maya) of racism and tribalism. There will be no gravitation to such primitive and uncivilized belligerent behavior. Communities will be more hospitable and neighborly. There will be no need for social ambitions, status seeking, keeping up with the Joneses, concerning oneself with the way one is seen by others and the distorted way one sees others. The focus of individuals will be on seeing, by analyzing oneself and discovering the revelations of their higher conscious selves, instead of today's normality of the dysfunctional and torturous practice of concerning oneself with only how one is always being seen.

Environment

Our planetary environment will also be heavily impacted. Communities will have an awareness of self and awareness that self also means all there is. To be one with all there is means to see yourself as all there is, including the environment of the planet. Communities will be environmentally friendly, from the construction of buildings, the industry of agriculture, transportation, chemical manufacturing, and to industrial processing.

Population management will play a role in the practice of environmentalism, for humans and animals. Animal conservationism will be more advanced.

Animal rights activists will begin to realize the progressive affects that mental health and wellness treatments for all people will have on the welfare of animals.

Activists from all environmental and social movements will immediately begin to recognize the changing of all hearts, minds and the effect that the cause of mental health and wellness treatments for all will have on the outcome toward matters they advocate for. Stacey Abrams wrote the best seller, *Our Time is Now*, which gives us the insight that we need to sustain change. Well, here is how we do it: a mental health and wellness treatment system for all will sustain change.

Political Climate

The political climate we are experiencing today will be considered unprecedented and through the measures of time will be rectified, through the system of treatments for all. Through rectified treatments, one will be nudged toward being allowed to evaluate and understand the factors of the ego, in order to uncover the ego's collective, mental and low morale characteristics. The purpose of deliberating and disclosing the scientific, spiritual and psychological awareness of the ego is to uncover that the unattended-to ego may hinder one's ability to perceive truth and reality, to obtain and thrive through our human journey of intelligence and communications. A considerate seeking and practicing of scientific, spiritual growth of awareness of the ego will permit a politician to see their own egotistical mishaps. Perhaps it will result in their capacity to accumulate the ideals and the competence of finding solutions to problems, to unearthing more adequate and advanced ways to administer humanity's goals, visions and purpose toward our next stage in evolution.

Every aspect of mental, spiritual and physical science must lead our way of life, beginning with mental essentials. That implies the importance politicians have with regard to the willingness to assert the science to correct our dysfunctional and mental conditions that we all have a common interest in. In this way, every community will experience the functional outcomes that will amount to a balance in human decency and respect for each other. Developments of human decency and respect through systematic treatments will at last give politicians the ability to exhibit the qualification and ideals to apply real, careful and precise political checks and balances.

There will be no such thing as political defeat or political deadlock. Every ideal will have a scientific assessment. Politicians will have an authentication and be disentangled from the corruption and greed of today's politicians. Mental wellness treatments for all could direct our democracy away from campaign finances, super PACs, corporate lobbyists and many factors that have a hand in our current political gridlock. Mental health and wellness treatment for all is the remedy for political gridlock.

Politicians of a mental health and wellness treatment system for all will have the insight through treatments to know and understand the importance of the science that economic security for all is key to having a thriving democracy and society.

Politicians of tomorrow will have the conviction and perception to comprehend the importance of functional societal establishments and the inspiration to have thriving civilization achievements.

They will understand the importance of the augmentation of cosmic knowledge and science of all sorts, especially spiritual science.

They will understand the importance of health care and disease prevention for all, including mental health and wellness treatment for all.

They will understand the importance of education for all and the protection of the stability of families.

They will understand the importance of individual liberties for all, and mandatory employment of respect for all life.

They will understand the importance of all-around racial impartiality and equality, and the importance of compassion and care for the unfortunate.

Economics

Socioeconomic elements will be more parallel and impartial to one's personal satisfaction. Economic security will appear in the form of individuals paying and donating contributions to one another for their wisdom and intellectual insight. Industrialization will be wiser and intellectual in developments and manufacturing, due to our transparency of mind that will transpire from a system of treatments. Economic security will be embodied and centered by way of a mental health and wellness treatment system for all. As an example, let's say you find any kind of job—you're given a probationary period that should consist of a compulsory stable amount of therapy, regarding to that probationary time. Perhaps one should periodically maintain one's therapy throughout the duration of his or her employment.

Social elements of the workplace will be sacred to unify, respect and communalize oneness. Safety in the workplace would be willfully applied. Commemorations and celebrations will be allocated to the workplace. The display of love and respect will be universal, displayed everywhere and unavoidable.

No more housing and business banking inequality. Banking and taxes and corporate encounters will be of respect, dignity and balance. The conventional banking practices of restricted disclosure fraud and redlining discrimination according to race and poverty stricken neighborhoods will be unheard of and outrageous. Taxes will be an even-handed triumph and everyone will engage in their fair share comfortably. Greed will be a thing of the past for many in today's society who view tax paying for those who are well off as burdensome. Corporate corruption will be abolished, through the checks and balances between mental health and wellness treatments and lawmaking politicians, whose job will be based on not only ideas and problem solving, but also the measure of their own mental soundness. Perhaps they will lead by an example in willful participation of their own systematic wellness treatments. Perhaps society advocates and establishes a peremptory request of mental health wellness treatment as an incentive to be a politician or any other occupation.

Science

Economics will endure some progressive impacts through science. There will be communities in the science world that will be more correlated and balanced due to mental health and wellness treatments for all. The evolution of science will be innovative and palpable in agronomy and food production, transportation, housing, communication network systems, space, and planetary dimensional exploration. Science will soon discover that when the world has gone mad, we are to give therapy to the world. Health care will finally be a right for all and will finally reach advance scientific and technological heights. Life expectancy will scientifically result in a tremendous increase.

Entertainment of all sorts will be able to merge through the improvements of science and will be capable of achieving intelligible apexes.

For instance, imagine vivid, tangible, even more highly advanced artificial intelligent light or dark life simulations one can experience—for the purpose of exploration, adventure, teaching, studying, and discovering for the aim of spiritual growth, mental health treatment, scientific research and development. Picture the amalgamation of sports and entertainment of all kinds, coming together through a compelling evolutionary impact of humanity's scientific aptitude, contributed by the effects of a universal mental health and wellness treatment system for all.

This will be feasible not to just any random treatment system, but a treatment system that will be productively implemented with precision.

Spiritual Science

Spiritual science is a knowledge of the nature and laws of existence involving consistent systematized observation of the methods of conscious movement, through the spiritual nature of all aspects of absolute existence.

The practice of spiritual science will secure the vantage point that will carry out the refurbishment of all institutions and factors of societies and will be humanity's underlying principle for integrity and temperament. The consolidation of spirituality and science, and not corrupt religion under limited interpretations, will inevitably elevate in all matters of our human experiences. For an example, the integration of spirituality and science will have its ultimate effect on our mental health and wellness treatment methods and conditions. The system of treatment for all will be the seed of our civilization. Although we must first repent, how do we repent? We repent by changing the way we view and think of our world that created the mental paralysis we are all currently experiencing. How do we change the past views and thinking? We change them by exercising the changing of mind, view and thinking with mental wellness treatment. It is simple science. Like mentioned before, spirituality is a science ruled by laws just like other branches of science, along with its observational and methodical evidence in experiences and results.

Spiritual science will influence all aspects and institutions of societies, because humanity will inherit an evolutional leap, from the third dimensional existential perspectives and experiences to the fourth, fifth, and so forth, through experiencing it as so. This inevitable possibility incorporates an evolutional trickle-down effect in the faculties of telepathy teleportation, the capacity to heal, and to exert life expansion, et cetera. It is very complex for one to assimilate under a third dimensional state and perspective. To comprehend such an evolutional possible leap, one must motion and mature toward the progression of a fourth dimensional state and perspective, through the meditative practice of self-reflecting on the psychology of universal laws and principles of the higher self.

The evolutional escalation in spiritual science improvement will lessen the esteem of individuality in the sense of only identifying one's self with the human body, and the I, me and my lower egotistical perspective of oneself. Individualism will reside among third dimensional humans, but as one dwells and advances toward universal and cosmic states of perspectives of paradise or nirvana (absolute state of being), it will allow our world to subside from our current burdensome, delusional state to reaching our highest point of spiritual science and self-awareness, as seeking and dwelling ascended human beings. Due to the primary purpose of spiritual science and self-awareness seeking and dwelling sort of human beings, it will be all about being in oneness with the universe (God), through the lens and practicing of a pantheistic perspective, of seeing the universe (God) in and as all there is, in every aspect of our existential experiences. Every individual will be perceived as one's own self in another lifetime and in another life form.

We will all conclude that we all have the same consciousness, and that there is only one consciousness. This one consciousness that we all share, and that we call God, the Universe, the Cosmos, the Absolute, et cetera, will finally be perceived by all as, the self, because we will all finally know, that we all have and are the all consciousness.

From this particular knowing, we will propel humanity into the fulfillment of universal consciousness (Christ Consciousness) and prophetic prophecies from many prognosticators, into becoming unified as one man and living the purpose of the universe. The purpose for humanity is to become one with all energies, forces and entities of the universe.

The purpose and future of humanity will be returning to a state where we once were, but have no recollection of, which is designed by universal law.

So here is a reasonable premonition, on a logical perspective of who we were and why, by universal law, we are for the most part unable to remember past states of being.

As mentioned before, we are all imperishable spirits having a human experience. We have been existing with and as consciousness for eternity. With that said, universal law forbids us for the most part the capability to remember our past states in this life. Just imagine being able to remember multiple loved ones from past lives. How in the world will you learn the lessons purposely intended and imperative to learn in this life?

The reason for this forbidden law is to spare us from the heartaches from past experiences of attachments and the unbearable mental anguish that would disable this life, so that we may accomplish purposeful goals in this life.

The evidence of this perspective dwells in the experiences of consciousness by the expressions of déjà vu, or vivid intuitional dreams and strong thought—the fact that it is impossible to extinguish a spirit and soul in which we all possess will say so. If we have existed for all times and we are eternal and indestructible spirits and souls, then we all possess the experiences and memories of our essence and of whom we are all truly beyond this lifetime.

The nature of a system of precise treatments will put humanity on a path of eradicating the veils that sabotage our intrinsic understanding of the spirit and soul, consciousness and the evolved higher self. A mental health and wellness treatment system for all will catapult us all in our original return to the state of mental Eden, where the possibilities of humanity will be indescribable, unlimited and just. It will be Heaven on Earth, as it is in Heaven.

The Outcome

So What?

     So what are we to look forward to? What collective stand will we all take? To what measure will we, society, urge countermeasures and a cure to our current collective encumbrance of mental instabilities and conditions? What will we demand of ourselves? What will we demand of each other? What will we demand from our lawmakers? What will we choose to determine as the outcome of our ongoing holistic, mental incompatibilities and the prolongation of such a jointed state of being? Will we be able to shift national and international discussions toward a more progressive analytical take on the concept of mental health and wellness treatments for all, as the principal item for all of humanity?

Mental Eden (God)

Mental Eden: a state of universal and cosmic awareness of one's absolute self, as all things and all existence. One's highest reality and changeless truth, that results in a balance of mind, peace and elation.

Will we know Nature & Laws?

Will the outcome be as though humanity has finally connected to the importance and distinctions of nature and its laws and the ability of the connecting of dots? The ability to administer what particular universal law will apply, with whatever circumstantial aspect of an encounter with one's experiences in this existence and with nature, and understand the right relationships between things? Will we develop the capacity to cultivate the respect that is essential to nature and its laws?

Will we know Love?

Will the outcome look as though humanity has expanded the perspectives of love? Will we see the nature of ourselves as love, because we are love? We are all the nourishments of life, because we are the love that creates ourselves.

Will we know Spirit & Soul?

Will the outcome dwell in the form of the improvements of our human comprehension that nature's applied law of love is the spirit (the character) experienced as memory that is consciousness, that connects to human feeling, which is also known as the soul? Will we secure and discriminate the sentiments toward the truthful descriptions of spirit and soul by way of experiencing its persona, and not just by blind belief?

Will we know the Ego?

Will the outcome dwell as though our attentiveness to the comprehension of the human ego has inferred a more serious impact on our massive awareness of the ego? Will we eventually see the lower ego as the delusion that sees the self as the individual, and everyone else as other? The ego that only causes one to belittle and lie to oneself and see oneself as unworthy or inferior or superior? To see only mistakes and faults in oneself and others, that cause one to compare themselves with others? Will we overcome the ego that continues to rate itself, judge itself and others?

Will we know the lower ego and self that identifies with the mind, body, senses, and also known as the veil of suffering? Will we know the lower ego that deludes the nature of one's true self, which generates the effect of human suffering?

What will be the outcome of humanity's choice to continue on the path of practicing the normalization of the unrestrained ego? Will the outcome appear to treat, confine and remedy the dysfunctional practices of the unbalanced ego, in the direction of our evolutional highest reality of mental Eden?

What will become of our Product of Environment?

Will the outcome of our emergence from the submersion of centuries of being a product of the environment of the oppressed and the oppressor—one that has the consequence of depression—

transform and heal all of our curses? Will we abolish the curse contracted from slavery known as the superiority complex? Will it find its dissipation and ruin? Will the outcome of a mental health and wellness treatment system for all be the seed of African-American reparations? Without a system that would target the mental discrepancy that has lured such prehistoric behavior, such practices will be prone to proceed and could be the cause of the extinction of humanity.

What will be of the System of Belief?

Will the outcome reveal itself as the endpoint of a system of belief, that transforms to the practice of spiritual perception? Perception according to the evidence of what one experiences and not indiscriminately believed because of a traditionally inherited condition—that is, conditioned without an intuitional or super reasonable experiencing of the truth and the complexions of one's true cosmic self.

Will we Reflect on Solutions?

Will the outcome exhibit our ability to reflect on solutions, and to generate effective ideals through meditative contemplation?

Do we have a Will to Choose to Act?

Will the outcome manifest a will to choose to act and overcome our collective mentally dysfunctional paralysis, instead of allowing our current leaders to possess the right of way to lead while they display, for all to see, their symptoms of mental defects? Will we enter into an expanded perspective that reasonably sums up the explanation that a system of mental health and wellness treatments for all could be pivotal to our collective mental stability?

What will be the Outcome of Mental Health and Wellness Treatment of the Past & Present?

Will the outcome of mental health and wellness treatments of the past and present carry on as torturous and absurd faulty science? Will we, as in many cases, resume in the way we take care of the mentally unsettled, with mentally unsettled practices and operations? Will we continue to allow institutions to plague the public with mentally galvanizing energies? Allowing penitentiaries to warehouse human beings in very savage environments of race riots, which fundamentally bares an equivalence and association to racial disparities in society? Will we allow prison institutions to provide very little or no reformatory treatments?

What will the Outcome Look Like?

Will the outcome look like we have put an end to personal ego centrical diagnosis? Ego centrical diagnosis toward heinous criminal mischief, according to the personal effect it bestows on one's personal mental incompatibility, so that we may begin to see that a criminal act is never committed by individuals who are of sound mind (sane), no matter what crime is committed?

How will we Improve?

Will we decisively and willingly choose to live up to our truthful potential and purpose, to raising standards on what we consider mentally unbalanced behavior or a state of mind, in order to secure our next evolutionary leap to universal and cosmic consciousness and raptured infinite bliss?

A Final Dialogue

The Bliss

The bliss is the most quintessential feature of the immortality of infinity. Its power and characteristics are seen in the third dimensional lower mind as something psychotic that defies the lower ego's human logic of dualism. Infinite bliss is the essence of who and what we are, and is what we will one day discover we are. The bliss and we are beyond time and space. Humanity has come from the bliss and will return to the bliss. Though at the same time, in the absolute sense of the subject, humanity has never left the bliss, since it is impossible to leave what we are. The bliss is the light (the knowledge) and love that we all experience. The bliss is existence itself—the cycle of life and death is conducted by the bliss. Whether you are interested or not, our journey is to reconnect to our original and ancient absolute self (the bliss/God).

Fourth Dimension

A logical footstep in such a direction as the fourth dimension would consist of the development of fourth dimensional perspectives. In order to advance to fourth dimensional perspectives, one must encounter the practice of mental balance with treatments of mental health and wellness remedies. The third dimensional perspectives that we practice are the perspective of practicing dualism. The fourth dimensions are the practicing observations of the universal laws of self-realization that go beyond dualistic perspectives, exercised from day to day as a paramount requirement to fourth dimensional results. It is not a matter of reaching fourth dimensional conscious measures because it is already there within you. It is only a matter of realizing the perspective laws of realizing one's true self. Mental health and wellness treatments have great potentials to initiate evolutionary perspectives of the fourth dimension and beyond, to the absolute cosmic self.

To Recognize and Insure the Collective Conditions

We currently insure many material objects and items, including our homes, vehicles and our physical body, health and wellbeing, that affect many elements of our lives and the lives of others. Though we have yet to see and comprehend the relevance of how we mentally and psychologically affect ourselves and the lives of others, and how much more important it is to insure our mental health and wellbeing than it is to insure our material possessions. Why aren't we building mental health care and treatment systems for all incentives, in order to possess our material possessions—perhaps a house, a vehicle and even our businesses and jobs? This is how we would induce a mental health care system for all. Just as we do in order to drive a vehicle, we establish compensation to make up for damages and loss with insurance policies. Damages and loss occur with mental discrepancies of a drunk driver so why aren't we insuring to ensure against our mental discrepancies? Why aren't we insuring our mental state, since our mental state does more damage than an object or vehicle and is the cause of all of our atrocities? Our mental state is central to every action we make and what influences those actions. They say you can't legislate hate, and I say you can: through a mental health care and wellness treatment system for all, with the cause of building a mental health and wellness treatment system incentive in order to possess material possessions to the effect that results in a sublime gradual success.

This is not someone's idiosyncratic enigma of what is taking place currently with our collective mental state and what is needed to eradicate such collective conditions. This is a matter that we all can see and experience before us, that results as such and that we all can conceive and ascertain as such. A system of mental health and wellness treatments for all, could be understood as not only imperative to where we are collectively at, but also as a rational approach to the cure of humanity's psychotic collective conflicted mental extravaganza.

The Mental State of the Opioid Epidemic

Just take a look at the unrelenting drug distributors. Could a reasonable and stable mind distribute the amount of opioids distributed across a nation of moribund opioid addicted citizens? Could reasonable and stable minded lawmakers allow such a senseless crisis to transpire among society as long as it has been permitted? Could reasonable, sound-minded lawmakers allow drug company owners to price hike their drugs for as long as it has been going on, so that citizens whose lives that depend on such drugs, won't have the means to afford such drugs to survive?

Assessments

A mental health and wellness treatment system for all will have a more achievable and plausible chance to avoid the next imminent threat of an insurrection sided by fallacies and conspiracy theories. Such a system can help us avoid the next commercial airline pilot from flying an aircraft full of passengers, perhaps while drunk and intoxicated. Such a system can prevent the next law enforcer from the horrific position of choosing to play judge, jury and executioner, or even just to protect law enforcers from mentally disturbed individuals. When institutions and human beings behave unreasonably, unstably and unsoundly, one may think that one would simply assess such a condition as unreasonable, unstable, and unsound, and determined to apply the restorative measures of mental health and wellness treatments. Such an assessment could even be determined by a five-year-old. However, the veil of the ego's positions, ambiguities and deceptions are to block such assessments. A mental health and wellness treatment system for all should be competent enough to tend to, renounce and subdue the complexities of the ego.

Mental Affect on Broadening Demands to Issues

Currently there has been a more intensified discussion on the issue of equal pay for all women. The demand for equal pay for women is merited. Though merited, the actual demand itself may require a more broadened demand in order to achieve attainable lasting satisfying conclusions. To implement an equal pay bill without a broaden equality demand that would target poverty would be an inefficient settling of an issue that will need a more expanded solution. To implement a bill that would be detailed enough to abolish the matter of poverty would be inefficient without addressing matters of equal pay, and many other issues that are linked to the causes of equal pay, like poverty. The issues of equal pay and the matter of abolishing poverty, and all other issues of human concern, should require endless and thorough psychoanalysis to certain satisfaction and societal progress.

All human issues of interest should possess a mentally balanced approach to what we have in common. A mental health care system for all is where we can go from here. The implementation of a capable system of mental health and wellness treatments, can launch humanity to rational and national resolutions in the manner of how we reach resolutions. Oprah Winfrey's discussion on "Where Do We Go From Here" with black thought leaders, activists and artists, in reference to the shameful crisis of systemic racism and the current state of America, which was a well needed discussion with only the missing central part and component of the matters of the discussion.

Perhaps here is the answer to that question: we can have a mental health and wellness treatment systems for all if we can mentally humble ourselves enough to champion, assemble, support and apply such a system.

Civil Societies

Why allow the status quo of our collective mental conditioning to be as it is, with the prevalence of depression or PTSD (Post Traumatic Stress Disorder) continuing to paralyze humanity's evolutional leap with nature? Why? Why are we doing nothing to address our systemic mental contradictions? Our collective mental disharmony is the seed of our current condition. We must heal the seed to heal the condition.

We view ourselves, as a civilization, to have an advanced stage or a system of social development. However, are we civilized when we deprive education and equal opportunity education to those less fortunate?

Would a civilized people resume the position of law-enforcement corruption? There have been a number of scandals involving many police departments but one in particular is the Philadelphia Police Department, who reprimanded, suspended and discharged numerous law-enforcement officers, allegedly exposed of inappropriate behavior. Many were in Facebook groups that were filled with varying types of hateful posts in regards to anti-Islamic speech, racial slurs of brutality with regards to African-American citizens, and rape memes including one geared toward congresswomen, et cetera. This systemic mental contradiction of swearing to protect the citizens, while simultaneously displaying and revealing mental discrepancies of hatred towards the actual citizens one swore to protect, unveils to reasonable and stable minds the moral mental deterioration of law-enforcement, and presents one of the main causes of police brutality that many citizens were always aware of. The Philadelphia Police Department unveils to reasonable and stable minded citizens and lawmakers across the world and the nation a compelling reason to reevaluate all police departments. The actress Kristen Bell referenced that we are all sameness, but we are going to need a mental wellness care system to recognize this sameness. A mental health and wellness treatment system for all can, and will, make a difference.

The Mental Position of Religious Cult Practices

There is a religious magazine, which I do not wish to disclose the name, where a writer wrote an article about why God gave Miriam, the sister of Moses, such a harsh punishment. The writer wrote that Miriam criticized Moses to his older brother Aaron in hopes of rectifying the situation of Moses marrying an Ethiopian black woman, as though Moses marrying a black woman was in need of being rectified. The writer mentioned that God was displeased with Miriam because she confided in Aaron and that Miriam's behavior was "meritorious."

The judgment of God is always in a human being's intent. In my opinion, the writer who wrote this article clearly sees nothing wrong with this racist and distorted interpretation, that Miriam's dissatisfaction with Moses marrying a black Ethiopian woman was some sort of meritorious act of honor.

Remember—this particular writer wrote this article in a religious magazine, as though in my view, it's a routine practice of this writer's distorted racist perspective. This distorted perspective in one's assessment is a depiction of a mentally unstable disposition that many encounter in many measures in today's societies. The mental catastrophes in our world make the argument that society itself could go for systemic mental reconciliation.

Have a Discussion

Our cognizance of the importance of dealing with mental health and wellness has evolved quite a bit. Nevertheless, there is still a sense of inconsequentiality and the lack of urgency to react, and to develop the requisite cognizance of mental health and wellness treatments and the attentiveness to detect, treat, manage and heal mental distortions.

Many consider guns to be the primary discussion of public shootings or of violence in general, which is true and is substantially viewed as a matter that plays a crucial part in the epidemic we are witnessing today. Though to engage in discussions of such sorts would lack in logic, if the "foundation" of such discussions of mental health and wellness treatments for all were not at the forefront. To get ahead of violence is to ensure a mental health and wellness treatment system for all.

Just think of humanity's current collective disposition and predicament. Just think of a great portion of the planet, along with your very own child in jeopardy of being exposed to a toxin that may one day cause their demise. Would you allow your child to partake in such a risk, or would you give it your all to protect your child? I believe one would give it their all to protect their child.

So I now ask the question, "why are we all allowing our current collective dispositions of mental conflicts to reside among us, while the threat of nuclear war and total annihilation lingers over the very existence of humanity?" We know it will take mentally unstable individuals to partake in such a grave tumultuous undertaking and we all can detect capable deranged world leaders, who live among humanity at our present moment, who could initiate the extinction of humanity. An "all hands on deck" approach of a mental health and wellness treatment system for all must be imperative. Teachers, pastors, government administrators, and citizens of all sorts should perhaps relinquish all pride and egotism and lead by an example for such a well deserving planetary shifting advancement. The question is: are we tired of the status quo?

Mental health and wellness treatments and rehabilitations FOR ALL is a key remedy that is identified and described through the science of spirituality. An automatic key to our woes and the next step toward humanity's next stage of evolution. The question is, will we look into the possibilities of the natural effects of the approach of mental health and wellness treatments for all, to achieve our next evolution, as the *Keys To Our Woes*?

Let's have a dialogue.

Statistics

The National Institute of Mental Health (NIMH) and the U.S. Dept. of Health and Human Services state that depression affects all age groups. Depression is one of the most common mental disorders in the U.S. Depression is a serious illness that affects one's thoughts, feelings, and ability to function in everyday life.

Bipolar disorder (also known as manic-depressive illness). While distinct from depression, it is characterized by periods of depression alternating with episodes of mania. It is present when a person experiences an abnormally elevated mood, less need for sleep, increased talkativeness, racing thoughts, distractibility, agitation and engaging in risky activities (e.g., spending a lot of money, reckless sex).

Symptoms and types of depression:

1) Persistent sad, anxious, or "empty" feelings
2) Feeling of hopelessness or pessimism
3) Feelings of guilt, worthlessness or helplessness
4) Irritability, restlessness
5) Loss of interest in activities and hobbies once pleasurable, including sex
6) Fatigue and decreased energy
7) Difficulty concentrating remembering or making decisions
8) Insomnia, early-morning wakefulness, or excessive sleeping
9) Appetite and/or weight changes
10) Thoughts of death or suicide, or suicide attempts

11) Aches or pains, headaches, cramps, or digestive problems that do not ease even with treatment

A diagnosis of major depressive disorder (or clinical depression) is made if an individual reports experiencing five or more of these symptoms in the same two-week period. Available treatments can alleviate symptoms, but many depressed people and those around them still fail to realize that they have an illness or could benefit from medical help.

Treatments for depression: Depression can be treated by medication, psychotherapy, or a combination of the two. Antidepressants influence the functioning of certain neurotransmitters in the brain. The most popular antidepressants are selective serotonin reuptake inhibitors (SSRIs). Serotonin and norepinephrine reuptake inhibitors (SNRIs) and bupropion are also commonly prescribed, as they have fewer side effects than drugs from old classes, such as tricyclics, tetracyclics, and monoamine oxidase inhibitors (MAOIs). Some people respond better, however, to the older antidepressants.

NIMH research has shown that certain types of psychotherapy, particularly cognitive-behavioral therapy (CBT) and interpersonal therapy (IPT), can help relieve depression. CBT helps patients change the negative thinking and behaving patterns often associated with depression.

IPT focuses patients on working through personal relationships that may contribute to depression. Studies of adults have shown that a combination of psychotherapy and antidepressant medication is most effective in treating moderate-to-severe depression.

Electroconvulsive therapy (ECT) has been found effective in treating some cases of severe depression, particularly those who have not responded to other treatment. ECT involves producing a seizure in the brain of a patient under general anesthesia by applying electrical stimulation through electrodes placed on the scalp. Memory loss and other cognitive problems, though common side effects, are typically short lived. Other types of treatment involving brain stimulation are currently being studied.

Website: www.nimh.nih.gov

Acknowledgments

I gratefully acknowledge the following sources and authors for their quotes, insights, and references:

- Abrams, Stacey
  - Our Time is Now
  - Copyright 2020
  - Henry Holt and Company
- Bell, Kristen
  - The World Needs More Purple People
  - Copyright 2020
  - Random House Children's Books
- Bly, Nellie
  - Investigative journalist, writer, and inventor
  - Known for going undercover at Blackwell's Island Asylum that sparked reform of treatments of the mentally ill
  - 1864 -1922
- Cordovero, Rabbi Moses
  - Rosh Yeshiva and Judge
  - Known for contributing to Kabbalistic literature and thought
  - 1522 – 1570
- Fabian, Renee
  - Journalist and editor

- The History of Inhumane Mental Health Treatments, July 31, 2017
- Gladwell, Malcolm
  - Talking to Strangers
  - Copyright 2019
  - Little, Brown and Company
- Howe, Neil
  - Former contributor to Forbes Magazine
  - Millennials and the Loneliness Epidemic, May 3, 2019
- OpenStax: Psychology
  - Mental Health Treatment: Past and Present

I am also grateful to my editor, Tekky Andrew-Jaja, whose suggestions have made this book more personal and inviting. I want to also thank my book designer and formatter, Kool Designs, for bringing the book to life. Thank you also to anyone I've forgotten who was instrumental in this project.

www.ingramcontent.com/pod-product-compliance
Lightning Source LLC
Chambersburg PA
CBHW030024290326
41934CB00005B/472